THE PULSE

OF PROGRESS

Turning Chaos into Harmony, One Process at a Time

ASHOK TIWARI

INDIA • SINGAPORE • MALAYSIA

ISBN 979-8-89906-643-6

Contents

Chapter – Wise Unique Angles & Perspectives

📌 **INTRODUCTION: THE PROCESS MINDSET SHIFT**

Unique Angle: Most businesses fail not because of bad products but due to **broken processes**. This chapter redefines process mastery as a **growth enabler** rather than a compliance burden.

🚀 **PART 1: THE FOUNDATIONS OF PROCESS MASTERY**

1. **Process Thinking: The Hidden Superpower of Successful Businesses**

   Fresh Take: Explores how elite companies use process thinking to **gain a competitive edge**, with real-world success stories and failures.

2. **The Process Bottleneck Myth: Why More Effort ≠ More Results**

   Unique Angle: Debunks myths around "working harder" vs. **working smarter**. Uses real examples of teams burning out due to process inefficiencies and how small tweaks **can 10X efficiency.**

3. **Process vs. People: Finding the Perfect Balance**

   Engaging Twist: Many professionals blame "bad employees," but often, the **real culprit is a broken process.** This chapter will introduce **systems thinking** and how businesses can create high-performing teams **without micromanagement.**

◪ PART 2: DESIGNING PROCESSES FOR EFFICIENCY & GROWTH

4.   **The Process Mapping Framework: Turning Chaos into Clarity**

Unique Perspective: Introduces an easy-to-apply **Process Mapping Formula** (without jargon) using a **fictional business transformation story** as an example.

5.   **Automate, Delegate, Eliminate: The 3-Step Efficiency Formula**

Fresh Approach: Shows how **80% of business inefficiencies** come from processes that could be **automated, delegated, or removed** entirely. Includes practical checklists for professionals & business owners.

6.   **The Pareto Principle of Process Mastery: Fixing the 20% That Matters Most**

Insightful Twist: Focuses on the **80/20 rule in process management**, showing how businesses waste time fixing the **wrong things** while ignoring high-impact areas.

◉ PART 3: RISK-PROOFING & SCALING BUSINESS OPERATIONS

7.   **The Silent Profit Killers: Identifying Hidden Process Leaks**

Unique Perspective: Breaks down **Operational, Financial & Compliance Risks** in a relatable way, with real-world case studies where minor process errors led to **huge business losses**.

8.   **From Start-up to Scale-Up: Process Frameworks That Grow with You**

Fresh Take: Explores how **small businesses fail to scale** because they don't upgrade their processes at each growth stage. Includes **real case studies** of businesses that nailed it vs. those that collapsed.

9. **The Process KPIs: Measuring What Matters**

    Engaging Twist: Many businesses track too many **useless KPIs**. This chapter simplifies the **5 essential process KPIs** every working professional & business owner should track for **real impact**.

🏆 **PART 4: MASTERING THE ART OF CONTINUOUS PROCESS IMPROVEMENT**

10. **Process Mastery in Action: The 1% Rule for Exponential Growth**

    Unique Angle: Focuses on the **power of micro-improvements—** how just **1% daily process optimization** can lead to **huge business growth over time**.

11. **The Process Mastery Culture: Embedding Excellence in Teams**

    Fresh Perspective: Explores how organizations like **Google, Amazon & Toyota** have built **process-driven cultures**, making them **resilient & scalable**.

12. **The Future of Process Excellence: AI, Automation & Beyond**

    Forward-Looking Twist: Covers the **next-gen process tools**, AI-driven automation, and how businesses **must adapt or be left behind**.

Dedication

To the silent warriors of everyday excellence—

To my mentors, who taught me the value of structure.

To my colleagues and clients, who challenged me to grow.

To my family, whose unwavering support made this journey possible.

And to every reader who has felt overwhelmed by chaos but still chose to
show up and build—

this book is for you.

**May you find clarity in process, strength in structure, and
fulfilment in mastering your craft.**

Preface

Have you ever marvelled at how effortlessly the human body functions—day in, day out—without missing a beat?

Your heart, a relentless engine, pumps **over 100,000 times a day**, circulating **about 2,000 gallons of blood** daily, delivering oxygen and nutrients to every living cell. It does this without needing reminders, meetings, or an SOP document—it just *knows* what to do, and it *executes flawlessly*.

Your kidneys filter around **50 gallons of blood each day**, removing waste and maintaining the delicate balance of minerals and fluids—silently and efficiently, 24/7. The lungs, liver, brain, digestive tract—each organ plays its role with unwavering discipline, following a natural sequence, a precise rhythm.

This remarkable orchestration is nothing but a masterpiece of *process design*. A biological SOP, perfected by nature over millions of years. No chaos, no firefighting—just pure alignment, efficiency, and excellence.

NOW IMAGINE

What if your organization could work like that?

What if your business could function like a living organism—where every team, task, and system knows its role, flows in harmony, and contributes seamlessly to the health and growth of the whole?

If there's one thing that separates high-performing businesses from struggling ones, it's not just great products, talented teams, or cutting-edge technology—it's the mastery of processes.

Through my own journey, particularly during my training with a leading multinational corporation (MNC), I witnessed first-hand how creating Standard Operating Procedures (SOPs) and integrating the SIPOC (Suppliers, Inputs, Process, Outputs, Customers) model at each step of a process and sub process can fundamentally change an organization's understanding of efficiency and effectiveness.

In my years of working with different corporates, I've seen first-hand how organizations rise—or fall—based on how well they structure, optimize, and execute their processes. Some businesses thrive despite challenges, while others, with all the right resources, still struggle to stay afloat. What makes the difference? It's the ability to design, refine, and scale processes that create efficiency, reduce risks, and drive sustainable growth.

This book is not about theory. It's about action

Why This Book? Why Now?

The world of business is evolving faster than ever. Automation, AI, digital transformation, and regulatory shifts are reshaping industries. Yet, despite all these advancements, many professionals and business owners are stuck in the old ways of working—relying on ad-hoc decisions, firefighting issues, and reinventing the wheel instead of streamlining their systems.

This book is for those who are tired of inefficiency, chaos, and stagnant growth. Whether you're a corporate professional looking to enhance your productivity, a manager aiming to improve team performance, or a business owner striving to scale your operations, this book will serve as your roadmap.

What You'll Learn in This Book

Unlike traditional books on operations and management, *The Pulse of Progress* is designed to be practical, engaging, and actionable. Every chapter provides real-world strategies, proven frameworks, and easy-to-apply techniques that will help you:

✓ Identify & fix broken processes that are draining your time and profits.

✓ Automate, delegate, and eliminate inefficiencies using the 80/20 rule.

✓ Build scalable systems that support long-term business growth.

✓ Reduce operational, financial, and compliance risks by making smarter decisions.

✓ Leverage AI and automation to future-proof your processes.

This book is structured into four core sections:

★ *Laying the Foundations* – Understanding why process mastery is a game-changer.

★ *Designing for Efficiency & Growth* – Step-by-step frameworks to create streamlined, high-performing workflows.

★ *Risk-Proofing & Scaling* – Ensuring that processes support sustainable growth while minimizing risks.

★ *Continuous Improvement & Future Readiness* – Embedding a culture of efficiency and innovation.

Who Is This Book for?

This book is for corporate professionals, managers, entrepreneurs, and business owners who want to get ahead in their careers and businesses by mastering the art of process excellence. Whether you are scaling a Startup, optimizing corporate workflows, or leading a team, the strategies shared here will help you save time, cut costs, and maximize efficiency.

Final Thoughts

Mastering processes isn't about adding complexity—it's about simplifying success.

By the time you finish this book, you'll have the tools, mindset, and strategies to turn chaos into clarity, inefficiency into impact, and stagnation into scalable growth.

So, let's get started.

Your journey to Process Mastery begins now. 🚀

Introduction Note

Every great creation—be it a symphony, a skyscraper, or a thriving business—has one thing in common: a process behind the scenes that makes the magic happen.

When I first stepped into the corporate world, I was armed with ambition and curiosity. But very quickly, I realized that effort alone wasn't enough. It wasn't the loudest voice or the brightest idea that made a difference—it was the person who knew how to bring order to the chaos, who could create a roadmap where others saw roadblocks. That's when I fell in love with processes.

Over the years, I've come to believe this: **Processes are not about control—they're about clarity.**

They are not about bureaucracy—they are about breathing space.

They're what allow creativity to thrive, people to collaborate, and businesses to grow with confidence.

This book is not written from an ivory tower of theory, but from the trenches of boardrooms, client meetings, training rooms, and real-world experiences. It is shaped by the lessons learned through trial and error, wins and losses, simplicity and struggle.

My hope is that *The Pulse of Progress* doesn't just inform you—but inspires you. That you not only build better systems but live with more intention, purpose, and flow—just like the human body that inspires it all.

So here's to mastering the unseen gears that keep everything running.

To you—*the next Process Master.* Let's begin.

With heartfelt gratitude and a deep sense of purpose,

I dedicate this journey to **you**, the reader—because choosing to grow is the most powerful process of all.

Warm regards,

– Ashok Tiwari

Author, Coach & Process Evangelist

"Navigating Industry Challenges: Key Obstacles to Business Success"

As businesses navigate the complexities of their respective industries, they face a myriad of challenges that can hinder growth, efficiency, and overall success. Below, we outline the top common challenges that span various sectors, providing detailed insights into each issue. Understanding these challenges is crucial for developing effective strategies that drive process excellence.

- → Increasing Competition
- → Cultural shift due to technology
- → Regulatory compliance
- → Changing business models
- → Rising expectation
- → Customer retention
- → Security breaches
- → Continuous innovation

Increasing Competition: Competitors now face fewer restrictions due to technological advancements and globalization. Companies are challenged to continually innovate in order to stand out and offer something different. Moreover, intense competition often results in pricing conflicts which forces companies to incur lower costs without jeopardizing quality. At the same time, market leaders need to safeguard their market position with strong customer loyalty schemes and enhance relationships with existing customers.

Cultural Shift Due to Technology: Remote work, digital communication, and automation are becoming more common. These advancements require a change to management that fosters flexibility, and new skills adaptation. Additionally, organizations need to manage the concerns of employees regarding job elimination due to automation alongside the need to provide change through reskilling and upskilling programs.

Regulatory Compliance: Industries are subject to various regulations—ranging from data protection (e.g., GDPR) to industry-specific standards (e.g., healthcare, finance). Compliance requires ongoing education and investment in technology to monitor and implement regulatory changes. Noncompliance can lead to significant penalties and reputational damage, prompting businesses to establish dedicated compliance teams and integrate compliance into their organizational culture.

Changing Business Models: Traditional business models are being disrupted by innovation and consumer demand for convenience and personalization. For instance, the rise of subscription services, gig economy, and platform-based models challenge conventional sales and distribution channels. Companies must remain agile, leveraging data analytics and customer feedback to pivot their strategies and embrace new opportunities such as digital transformations and partnerships.

Rising Expectations: Customers expect personalized, seamless interactions tailored to their needs, driven by the experiences provided by leading tech companies. This requires businesses to utilize data analytics to anticipate and respond to customer preferences. Furthermore, there's a growing demand for transparency and ethical practices, pushing companies to commit to social responsibility and sustainable operations.

Customer Retention: Retaining customers is generally more cost-effective than acquiring new ones. Successful retention strategies include providing exceptional customer service, loyalty programs, and regular engagement through personalized marketing. Businesses benefit from leveraging feedback systems to continuously improve their offerings and address customer grievances promptly, building long-term relationships.

Security Breaches: As companies increasingly rely on digital infrastructures, they become targets for cyberattacks, which can compromise sensitive customer data, intellectual property, and operational systems. Businesses need to implement comprehensive cybersecurity strategies, including advanced threat detection, regular security audits, employee training on cybersecurity best practices, and incident response plans to mitigate risks.

Continuous Innovation: Innovation is crucial for staying competitive, requiring investment in research and development, fostering a culture of creativity, and encouraging cross-functional collaboration. Companies should tap into emerging technologies (e.g., AI, IoT) and be open to adopting innovative business practices. Engaging with external innovation ecosystems, such as Startup collaborations and industry partnerships, can also spur new ideas and accelerate growth.

The Heart of Business: Central Themes That Drive Success Across Industries

Every industry operates on a central theme that underpins its business activities and strategic initiatives. For instance, in the retail sector, the focus is on enhancing customer experience and inventory management, while in banking, the priority revolves around effective risk management and regulatory compliance. The pharmaceutical industry centres on maintaining strict adherence to regulations, ensuring product safety and efficacy. In healthcare, delivering exceptional patient care is at the forefront, whereas aviation prioritizes safety and operational integrity.

Recognizing these fundamental themes is crucial for companies as they develop their standard operating procedures (SOPs) and operational frameworks. By aligning their processes with these core themes, businesses can not only ensure compliance with industry regulations but also optimize their operational efficiency. This strategic alignment reinforces organizational performance and provides a competitive advantage in the marketplace.

For example, incorporating visual aids and checklists in retail operations can streamline inventory management and enhance accuracy. In banking, integrating risk management techniques into SOPs allows for the identification and mitigation of potential issues before they escalate. Similarly, in the pharmaceutical sector, aligning SOPs with regulatory standards ensures product integrity and fosters consumer trust.

As we delve deeper into these topics in the upcoming chapters, you will gain valuable insights into how various industries navigate their unique challenges. This understanding will equip you with the tools to manage the complexities of modern business processes effectively, leading to sustained success across different sectors. No matter the industry, embracing central themes in business operations is key to achieving and maintaining excellence.

1. **Retail Sector: Inventory Management and Stock Optimization**

   The retail industry struggles with maintaining optimal inventory levels, leading to either stock shortages or excess inventory. Effective inventory management is essential to meet customer demands while reducing carrying costs. Visual aids such as flowcharts, diagrams, and checklists can streamline this process, ensuring timely reordering and efficient stock management.

2. **Banking Sector: Risk Management Integration**

   In banking, risk management is a central theme, encompassing operational, financial, and compliance risks. The integration of robust risk assessment procedures into Standard Operating Procedures (SOPs) is essential. For instance, SOPs for loan processing must include processes for verifying borrower information and mitigating fraud, ensuring a secure lending environment.

3. **Pharmaceutical Sector: Compliance with Regulatory Standards**

   Pharmaceutical companies face stringent regulatory requirements that demand adherence to quality and safety standards. SOPs must align with guidelines established by regulatory bodies such as the FDA and EMA. This includes implementing comprehensive cleansing and sterilization protocols in drug manufacturing SOPs to satisfy mandatory regulations.

4. **Automobile Sector: Commitment to Continuous Improvement**

   The automobile industry thrives on continuous improvement through methodologies like Kaizen. Regularly updating SOPs based on performance metrics and employee feedback enhances operational efficiency. For example, assembly line SOPs benefit from worker input to identify incremental process improvements that streamline production.

5. **Information Technology Sector: Version Control and Documentation**

   In the rapidly evolving IT landscape, maintaining updated SOPs through a stringent version control system is vital. This ensures that all personnel access the most current processes. IT service management SOPs, for instance, necessitate detailed logs of process modifications to provide clarity and accountability.

6. **Healthcare Sector: Patient-Centric Care**

   In healthcare, the priority is patient safety and quality care. SOPs must implement evidence-based practices and detailed guidelines for critical tasks. Examples include preoperative checklists and postoperative care instructions, which aim to minimize risks and enhance patient outcomes.

7. **Manufacturing Sector: Lean Methodology Implementation**

   The manufacturing sector embraces this principle to increase efficiency and eliminate waste. SOPs should focus on streamlining processes to ensure each step adds value. Assembly line SOPs, for example, must address bottlenecks and reinforce seamless workflow processes.

8. **Aviation Sector: Stringent Safety Protocols**

   Safety is paramount in the aviation industry, necessitating stringent compliance with regulations. Comprehensive SOPs for pre-flight inspections are critical to ensuring all aircraft systems are thoroughly examined and verified before departure, safeguarding passenger and crew safety.

9. **Energy Sector: Environmental and Safety Compliance**

   The energy sector is bound by local and international environmental and safety regulations. SOPs must incorporate comprehensive protocols for environmental protection, emergency response, and the management of hazardous materials, ensuring compliance and sustainability in operations.

10. **Telecommunications Sector: Effective Change Management**

    Rapid technological advancements and evolving consumer demands require robust change management within the telecommunications industry. SOPs for network upgrades need to outline detailed procedures for planning, implementation, testing, and rollbacks, ensuring adaptability and responsiveness to change.

CHAPTER 1

Unlocking Success: The Power of Process Thinking

INTRODUCTION

In today's dynamic business world, failure is often attributed to factors like poor products or ineffective marketing. However, a deeper look reveals a more surprising truth: The overwhelming majority of business failures stem from a fundamental flaw—a lack of robust and well-managed processes. This chapter introduces the transformative power of process thinking, a methodology that shifts your perspective from isolated actions to interconnected systems, unlocking the path to sustainable growth and lasting success.

SECTION 1: UNDERSTANDING PROCESS THINKING

1.1. Redefining Business Success: From Outputs to Processes

Traditional business models often prioritize outputs: maximizing profits, boosting sales, achieving high customer satisfaction. While these are vital goals, focusing solely on outputs frequently overlooks the engine driving these results: the underlying processes.

→ **Results-First Approach (Negative):** This approach leads to firefighting—constantly addressing urgent problems without tackling underlying systemic issues. It results in short-term gains at the expense of long-term sustainability and scalability.

→ **Process-First Approach (Positive):** This approach focuses on designing, optimizing, and continuously improving the processes themselves. It leads to building efficient, repeatable, and scalable systems that drive sustainable success.

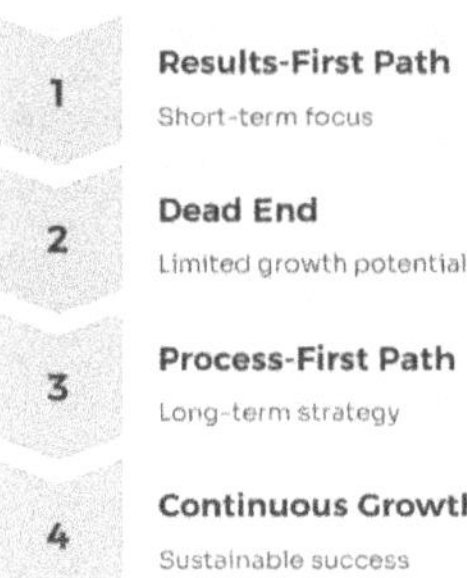

1.2. Process Thinking Defined: A Systems Perspective

Process thinking is a fundamental shift in perspective. It involves viewing tasks, workflows, and business functions not as isolated activities but as interconnected components within a larger system. By understanding the intricate relationships between these components, you can pinpoint inefficiencies, optimize workflows, and build a more resilient and adaptable business.

Business Process Interconnections

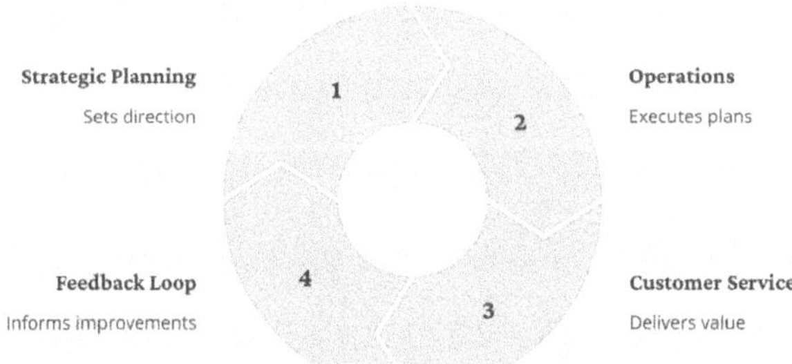

1.3. The McDonald's Model: Scalability Through Process Mastery

McDonald's serves as a prime example of process mastery. Their global success is not solely attributable to their menu but to the highly efficient, repeatable, and scalable systems they have built.

→ **Standardized Procedures:** Consistent procedures for food preparation, order taking, and customer service ensure predictable outcomes globally.

→ **Efficient Supply Chains:** Their carefully optimized supply chains ensure a consistent supply of high-quality ingredients to every restaurant worldwide.

→ **Quality Control:** Stringent quality control processes maintain consistency in product quality across all locations.

This combination allows McDonald's to scale effectively and efficiently across the globe.

SECTION 2: THE SCIENCE BEHIND PROCESS EXCELLENCE

2.1. Systems Thinking: Seeing the Big Picture

Systems thinking involves understanding the interconnectedness of various processes within an organization. Instead of viewing problems in isolation, systems thinking encourages examining the entire system to pinpoint the root cause of issues.

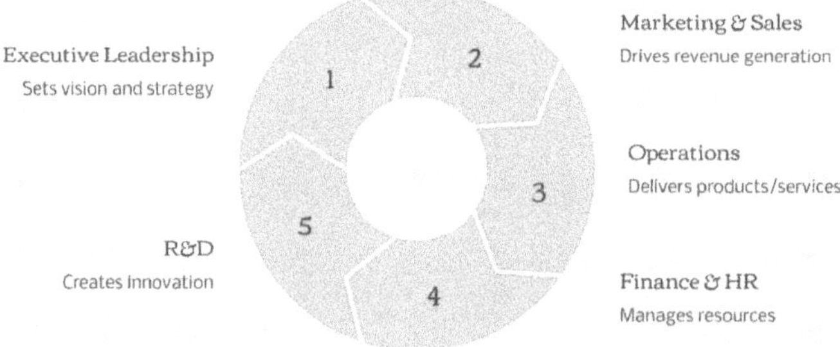

2.2. Leveraging Lean and Six Sigma Methodologies

These are powerful methodologies for optimizing processes. They share common goals of eliminating waste, enhancing efficiency, and improving quality control.

→ **Lean Principles:** Focus on eliminating waste in all aspects of production, reducing costs and improving efficiency.

→ **Six Sigma:** A data-driven approach to minimizing defects and errors in processes, improving consistency and reliability.

2.3. Overcoming Cognitive Biases

Often, intuition and overconfidence lead organizations to overlook systemic issues. Cognitive biases can prevent the recognition of underlying problems and the implementation of necessary changes. Awareness of these biases is crucial for successful process optimization.

→ **Confirmation Bias:** The tendency to seek out information that confirms pre-existing beliefs, ignoring contradictory evidence.

→ **Overconfidence Bias:** An inflated sense of one's abilities, often leading to a failure to seek external expertise or input.

→ **Anchoring Bias:** The tendency to overemphasize the first piece of information received, biasing subsequent decisions.

2.4. The Competitive Advantage of Process Mastery

Research consistently demonstrates that companies with well-documented and optimized processes outperform their competitors. By adopting a process-first approach, you can gain a significant competitive edge.

Companies with well-documented and optimized processes grow 30% faster than their competitors.

SECTION 3: REAL-WORLD EXAMPLES: SUCCESSES AND FAILURES

3.1. Success Stories

There are numerous inspiring success stories—ranging from Tata Steel, Hindustan Unilever, and Infosys —that clearly demonstrate the power of process thinking. These organizations have strategically embedded process excellence into their operational DNA, enabling them to adapt swiftly to evolving business landscapes.

Whether it was embracing digital transformation, optimizing supply chains, or streamlining internal workflows, these companies aligned their processes with the demands of the hour. As a result, they achieved remarkable outcomes—not just in terms of efficiency and innovation, but also in ensuring long-term sustainability and competitive advantage.

3.2 Failures as Lessons

- **Blockbuster vs. Netflix:** The failure to adapt to changing market dynamics due to rigid processes.

- **Kingfisher Airlines, Jet Airways:** The perils of rapid expansion without robust operational processes.

- **Satyam Computers:** The consequences of inadequate governance and internal controls.

- **Target Canada:** The risks of poor planning and untested supply chain processes.

SECTION 4: BUILDING A PROCESS-DRIVEN MINDSET

4.1. Identifying Core Processes

This section helps readers identify their critical business functions.

- → **Understanding Your Business Model:** Use a business model canvas as a visual aid.

- → **Prioritizing Processes:** Focus on those impacting customer satisfaction, revenue, and efficiency.

- → **Engaging Stakeholders:** Ensure a comprehensive view from different departments.

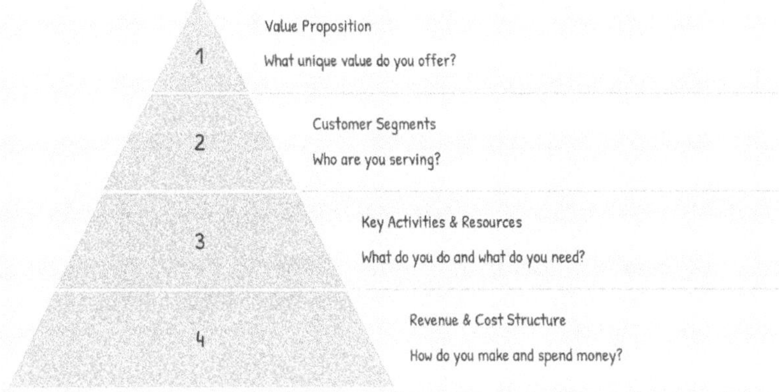

4.2. Optimizing Processes: Standardize, Automate, and Improve

- **Standardization and Optimization:** Remove bottlenecks and redundancies. Create detailed documentation (SOPs).

- **Automation and Scaling:** Leverage AI and software to automate tasks. Scale operations efficiently.

- **Continuous Monitoring and Improvement:** Use KPIs to track performance, identify areas for improvement, and continuously refine processes.

Let us summarize and understand the chapter through a beautiful story.

The Case of the Jittery Juice point

Once upon a time, in a bustling city, there was a juice point." They were known for their delicious, fresh juices, but their operations were, shall we say, chaotic. They were wildly popular, but the success was unsustainable. Orders got mixed up, ingredients ran out unexpectedly, and customers waited far too long. The owner, a passionate but disorganized entrepreneur named Zara, knew something had to change.

Zara's biggest problem was that, while she knew what to do, she couldn't clearly explain how things should be done to her employees. This resulted in inconsistencies, errors, and frustrated customers.

One day, a wise consultant named Professor Process came to Zara's rescue. Professor Process introduced Zara to two powerful tools: **Standard Operating Procedures (SOPs)** and **SIPOC (Suppliers, Inputs, Process, Outputs, Customers) analysis.**

Understanding SOPs

Professor Process explained that SOPs were like detailed recipes for every task in the juice point. They would provide step-by-step instructions for each process, ensuring that every employee performed their tasks consistently, correctly, and efficiently. For example, there would be an SOP for "Making a Mango Lassi," detailing exactly how much mango, yogurt, and ice to use, the exact blending time, and the correct serving temperature.

Understanding SIPOC and Its Integration with SOPs

Professor Process then introduced SIPOC, a framework for understanding the entire process, from start to finish. For the mango lassi, the SIPOC analysis would look something like this:

- → **Suppliers:** Mango farmer, dairy supplier, ice supplier

- → **Inputs:** Ripe mangoes, yogurt, ice, sugar, blending equipment

- → **Process:** (This is where the SOP steps would be detailed, from selecting ripe mangoes to serving the lassi.)

- → **Outputs:** Mango lassi (different sizes), sales data, customer satisfaction data, waste, etc.

- → **Customers:** Customers ordering at the counter, delivery drivers, etc.

Professor Process showed Zara how SIPOC and SOPs worked hand-in-hand. The SIPOC analysis provided the big picture; it showed where the processes started and ended and who was involved. Then the SOPs provided the detailed step-by-step instructions for every part of the process identified in the SIPOC. This clarity and standardization helped address several problems:

→ **Consistency:** Every mango lassi tasted the same, regardless of who made it.

→ **Efficiency:** Employees knew exactly what to do, eliminating confusion and wasted time.

→ **Improved Quality:** The process was standardized, reducing errors and improving product quality.

→ **Predictability:** Zara could better forecast ingredient needs and staffing levels.

→ **Scalability:** As the business grew, training new employees became much simpler because they were following detailed, proven procedures.

By integrating SOPs and SIPOC, The Juice point transformed from a chaotic business into a highly efficient, scalable, and customer-centric operation. Zara, finally stress-free, was able to focus on growing her business and delighting her customers.

This story effectively shows:

→ What SOPs and SIPOC are and their purpose.

→ How they complement each other.

→ The benefits of integrating them for streamlining operations.

"We will explore SIPOC and SOP in greater detail, along with their integration, as we progress through the upcoming chapters."

Quote: *"The strongest businesses aren't built on muscle—they're built on method."*

Quiz:

- True or False: Focusing solely on outputs (profits, sales) is the best way to ensure long-term business success.

- What is the main difference between a "Results-First" and a "Process-First" approach?

- True or False: Process thinking involves viewing tasks, workflows, and business functions as isolated activities.

CHAPTER 2

Beyond Hustle Culture: Unmasking the Myth of More Effort

INTRODUCTION

In today's business world, the "hustle culture" often dominates. The prevailing narrative suggests that working harder—longer hours, more staff, more resources—is the key to success. However, this chapter reveals a fundamental truth: Increased effort alone rarely solves business problems. True success lies not in overworking but in optimizing, identifying and eliminating the hidden process killers known as bottlenecks.

SECTION 1: THE HARD WORK TRAP: WHY MORE EFFORT OFTEN FAILS

1.1. The Hustle Culture Fallacy: A Misguided Approach

Many businesses operate under the misguided belief that simply working harder will inevitably lead to greater results. This "hustle culture" often overlooks the crucial role of efficient processes in achieving true success.

→ **The Illusion of Effort:** Increased effort does not automatically translate to increased output. Working longer hours or hiring more staff without addressing underlying process inefficiencies often leads to diminishing returns.

→ **The Law of Diminishing Returns:** Beyond a certain point, additional effort leads to burnout, errors, and decreased productivity. This ultimately undermines long-term success.

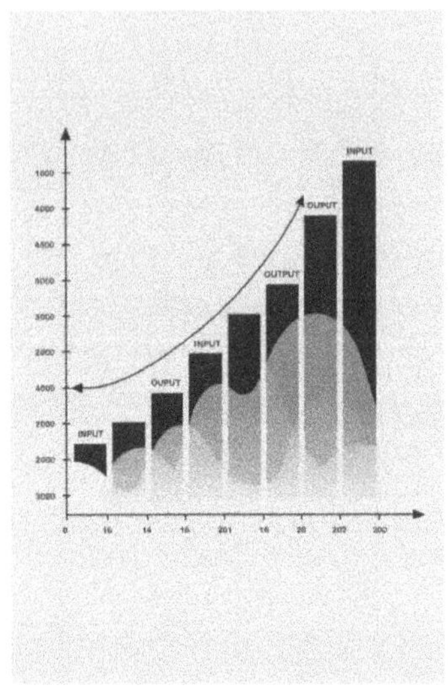

1.2. A Real-World Example: Amul's Milk Supply Chain Transformation

Before Amul revolutionized dairy processing in India, milk collection was scattered, unorganized, and inefficient, leading to high wastage and poor farmer income.

→ **The Problem:** Fragmented procurement process, lack of cold chain infrastructure, and inconsistent quality control.

→ **The Solution:** Amul implemented a cooperative model with standardized collection procedures, automated chilling centers, and a robust supply chain network. This drastically reduced spoilage, increased farmer earnings, and showcased the power of process optimization in rural India.

SECTION 2: UNDERSTANDING BOTTLENECKS: THE HIDDEN PROCESS KILLERS

2.1. Defining Bottlenecks: Constraints on Performance

A bottleneck is any constraint that limits overall performance. It's the single point in a process that slows everything down. Instead of simply pushing harder, successful businesses focus on identifying and resolving these bottlenecks.

2.2. Types of Bottlenecks

- **Capacity Bottlenecks:** Insufficient resources (staff, equipment, budget) relative to workload.

- **Decision Bottlenecks:** Slow approvals, excessive micromanagement, or lack of clear decision-making processes.

- **Process Bottlenecks:** Outdated workflows, excessive handoffs, or poorly designed procedures.

2.3. Real-World Examples: Identifying and Solving Bottlenecks

- **Hospital Emergency Rooms:** Inefficient patient triage and paperwork delays were the bottleneck, not a lack of doctors. The solution? Fast-track lanes and digital patient records.

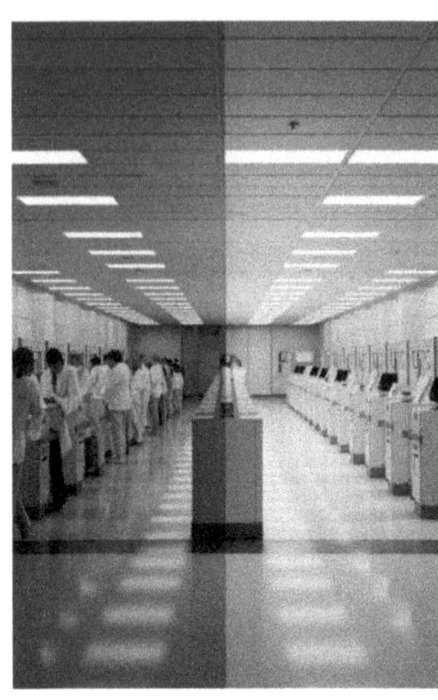

SECTION 3: THE 10X EFFICIENCY RULE: WORKING SMARTER, NOT HARDER

3.1. Identifying Process Loopholes

The Pareto Principle (80/20 rule) often applies to process inefficiencies: 80% of delays stem from just 20% of process flaws. Identifying and addressing these critical few flaws can have a dramatic impact on overall efficiency.

3.2. Case study - Amazon's Transformation: AI-Powered Efficiency

In early days, its warehouses were plagued by inefficient search processes. Their solution: AI-powered sorting and robotic picking, which cut fulfilment time significantly. This showcases the power of technology in eliminating bottlenecks.

Amazon Warehouse Evolution

Early Operations

Manual sorting and picking

Paper-based tracking systems

Limited automation

AI-Powered Today

Robotic fulfillment centers

Predictive inventory management

Automated sorting systems

3.3. Process Mapping for Clarity

- **Step 1:** Map the entire process to visualize the workflow.

- **Step 2:** Identify friction points (bottlenecks).

- **Step 3:** Apply automation, delegation, or elimination to resolve the bottlenecks.

Process Flow Visualization

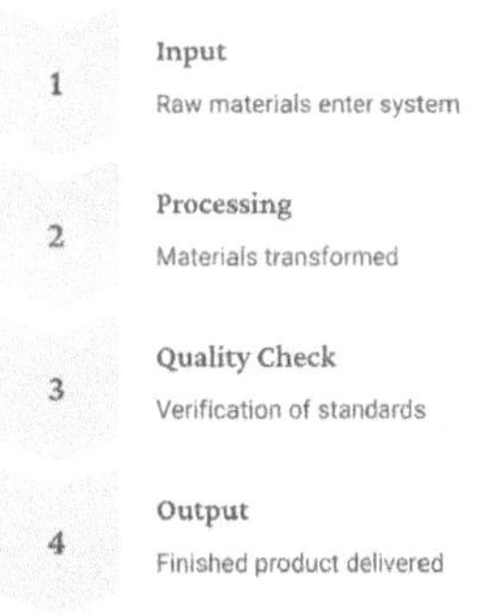

3.4. The Harvard Business Review Finding

Companies that identify and remove bottlenecks grow 40% faster than those that just hire more people.

SECTION 4: STRATEGIES FOR FIXING BOTTLENECKS: SMALL TWEAKS, BIG IMPACT

4.1. Automation: Automate repetitive tasks to reduce manual effort. Examples include Chabot's for customer service and automated data entry.

4.2. Delegation: Delegate tasks requiring human input but not necessarily your expertise. Examples include outsourcing non-core functions or using virtual assistants.

4.3. Parallel Processing: Run multiple tasks simultaneously instead of sequentially.

SECTION 5: KEY TAKEAWAYS AND ACTION STEPS

- Process bottlenecks are the root cause of inefficiency, not simply increased effort.

- Identify and eliminate bottlenecks before scaling.

- Small process tweaks can significantly increase efficiency (the 10X rule).

- Focus on optimization, not just overwork.

Continuous Improvement Cycle

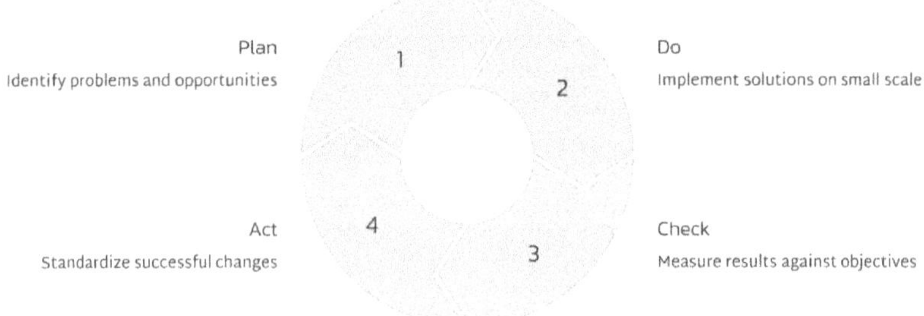

CLOSING STATEMENT

By embracing process thinking and implementing the strategies outlined in this chapter, businesses can build a robust process-driven culture that enhances efficiency, reduces costs, drives sustainable growth, and ensures long-term success.

"If you can't describe what you are doing as a process, you don't know what you're doing." – W. Edwards Deming

Let us summarize and understand the chapter through a beautiful story.

The Widget Wonder: A Story of Streamlined Production

"There was a medium-sized manufacturing company that produced small electronic widgets. They were struggling with high defect rates and slow production times. Their production line was a chaotic mix of manual processes, outdated equipment, and inconsistent procedures. Their factory manager, a seasoned worker named Alex, knew they had to improve efficiency, but he wasn't sure how.

A consultant introduced Alex to SIPOC and SOPs. They decided to focus on improving the assembly line. Here's their SIPOC map:

→ **Suppliers:** Parts suppliers (sensors, microchips, housings), packaging material supplier, equipment maintenance company.

→ **Inputs:** Individual parts, assembly equipment, workstations, trained personnel, quality control procedures, manufacturing instructions.

→ **Process:** (The detailed SOPs were developed for each stage of the assembly line):

- Parts delivery and inspection.

- Component assembly.

- Automated testing.

- Quality check and sorting (defective items separated).

- Packaging and labelling.

→ **Outputs:** Finished product, defect reports, production data, waste materials.

→ **Customers:** Distributors, retailers, end consumers.

Creating and meticulously following detailed SOPs for each step, combined with a SIPOC analysis, resulted in:

→ **Reduced Defect Rates:** Consistent procedures minimized errors.

→ **Faster Production Times:** Streamlined workflows increased output.

→ **Improved Quality:** Automated testing reduced errors and enhanced quality.

→ **Better Resource Management:** Clear procedures allowed for better allocation of personnel and equipment.

They experienced a significant turnaround, increasing their production efficiency and delivering higher-quality products. Alex, having learned the importance of robust processes, embraced SOPs and SIPOC for all factory operations.

Quote: *"You don't need to work harder—you need to stop leaking energy through broken systems."*

Puzzle:

- **Bottleneck Brainteaser:** Imagine a bakery where the oven can only bake 10 loaves of bread per hour, but the team can prepare 20 loaves per hour. What is the bottleneck, and how would you address it?

Quiz:

- What is a bottleneck in a process?

- Whether Increased effort always translates to increased output.

CHAPTER 3

High-Performing Teams: Prioritizing Processes Over People

INTRODUCTION

Many organizations struggle with performance issues, often attributing them to individual employee shortcomings. This chapter challenges that assumption, arguing that high-performing teams are not built solely on exceptional individuals but on well-designed and optimized processes. By shifting from a people-centric to a process-centric approach, organizations can unlock significant improvements in productivity, efficiency, and overall team performance.

SECTION 1: THE BLAME GAME: WHY PROCESSES, NOT PEOPLE, OFTEN FAIL

1.1. The Common Misunderstanding: Blaming Individuals

When things go wrong, the instinct is often to assign blame to individuals—labelling employees as "lazy," "unskilled," or "inefficient." However, this approach often overlooks the true culprit: a flawed process.

1.2. Recognizing the Root Cause: Broken Processes

Instead of focusing on individual failings, effective leaders identify and address the underlying systemic issues. This involves shifting from a people-centric to a process-centric approach, recognizing that broken processes, not individuals, are usually to blame.

- → **Example Scenarios:** (Remove the overly simplified examples of "lazy," "unskilled," "slow," replace with more compelling examples directly tied to process issues):

  - **Missed Deadlines:** Inadequate project management processes lead to missed deadlines, regardless of employee skill level.

  - **Quality Control Issues:** Poorly defined procedures cause inconsistencies in product quality.

  - **Low Morale:** Micromanagement and unclear expectations lead to low morale, impacting employee productivity.

1.3. Case Study: The Space Shuttle Challenger Disaster (Jan 1986)

The Challenger disaster tragically highlights the dangers of focusing on individual blame rather than addressing systemic failures. The initial investigation focused on engineer errors, but a more thorough review revealed a flawed decision-making process.

- → **The Root Cause:** Pressure to launch despite known safety risks, stemming from a flawed decision-making process.

- → **The Lesson:** Fixing the system (the process) is more effective than simply blaming individuals.

Info source: https://en.wikipedia.org/wiki/Space_Shuttle_Challenger_disaster

SECTION 2: SYSTEMS THINKING: A HOLISTIC APPROACH

2.1. Shifting Perspectives: Understanding Interconnections

Systems thinking encourages moving beyond individual failures to see how everything connects within a larger system. Every problem has a root cause within the system, and by understanding these connections, we can more effectively resolve issues.

2.2. Case Study: Call Centre Turnover

A call centre struggling with high employee turnover initially blamed individual employees for quitting. A systems thinking approach revealed a deeper problem: Repetitive work, lack of growth opportunities, and rigid scripts that frustrated both employees and customers. The solution was to empower agents with greater flexibility, better tools, and opportunities for growth.

→ **The Result:** A 40% reduction in employee turnover.

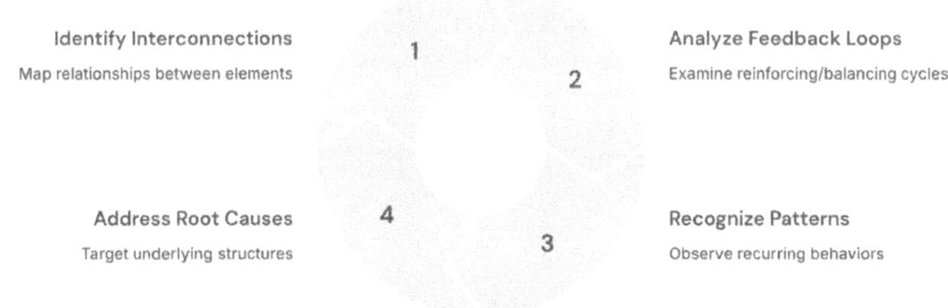

SECTION 3: PROCESS-FIRST LEADERSHIP: EMPOWERING TEAMS WITHOUT MICROMANAGEMENT

3.1. The Downside of Micromanagement

Micromanagement is counterproductive, killing productivity and creativity while undermining employee morale. It fosters a culture of fear and dependence, stifling innovation.

3.2. Process-First Leadership: A Better Approach

Process-first leaders focus on creating well-defined processes, empowering their teams, and fostering a culture of continuous improvement. They create effective systems where employees understand their roles, have the resources they need, and are encouraged to participate in improving processes.

→ **Key Elements:**

- **Clear Processes:** Document SOPs that clearly define roles, responsibilities, and procedures.

- **Smart Automation:** Implement automation to remove repetitive tasks and free up employees for more valuable work.

- **Feedback Loops:** Regular feedback sessions allow for continuous improvement and employee engagement.

3.3. Case Studies: Process-First Leadership in Action

- **Infosys:** Implemented a competency-based framework and detailed SOPs, improving employee retention and streamlining operations.

- **Flipkart:** Used AI-powered sortation systems and automated inventory management to streamline operations and improve customer satisfaction during peak seasons.

CLOSING STATEMENT

By embracing a process-first approach, businesses can create high-performing teams that are not only more productive and efficient but also more engaged and satisfied. This approach fosters a culture of trust, accountability, and continuous improvement—the keys to unlocking true business success. Remember, people don't fail—processes do. Fix the system, and success follows.

Let us summarize and understand the chapter through a beautiful story.

The Wellness Way: Optimizing Patient Care

"The Wellness Way" was a thriving health clinic known for its holistic approach to patient care. However, they struggled with long wait times, inconsistent treatment plans, and difficulties tracking patient progress. Their manager, Dr. Eva Rostova, a skilled physician, knew that improving their processes was critical for enhancing patient care and operational efficiency.

Dr. Rostova engaged a process consultant, who introduced her to the power of SOPs and SIPOC. They focused on optimizing their patient intake and treatment planning process. Their SIPOC analysis looked like this:

- → **Suppliers:** Referring physicians, medical equipment suppliers, laboratory services, insurance providers.

- → **Inputs:** Patient referrals, medical history, test results, insurance information, treatment plans, medical staff.

- → **Process:** (This section detailed the SOPs for patient intake, scheduling, consultations, treatment, and discharge):

  - Patient registration and initial assessment.

  - Scheduling appointments (optimizing appointment slots).

  - Medical consultations (following standard protocols).

  - Diagnostic testing (ordering and tracking results).

  - Treatment planning and implementation (based on evidence-based guidelines).

  - Progress tracking and follow-up.

  - Patient discharge and records management.

- → **Outputs:** Completed patient records, treatment outcomes, patient satisfaction scores, billing data.

- → **Customers:** Patients, referring physicians, insurance companies.

Implementing these SOPs resulted in:

- → **Reduced Wait Times:** Optimized scheduling and streamlined workflows significantly reduced patient wait times.

- → **Improved Treatment Consistency:** Evidence-based guidelines ensured consistent treatment plans.

- → **Enhanced Patient Satisfaction:** Improved communication and follow-up increased patient satisfaction.

→ **Better Data Management:** Standardized record-keeping improved data quality and accessibility.

The Wellness Way transformed its operations, improving both patient care and operational efficiency. Dr. Rostova, now a strong advocate for process-driven healthcare, continued to refine her clinic's processes.

Quote: *"Blaming people for process failures is like blaming the wheels for a broken engine."*

Quiz:

- Why is it important to focus on processes rather than blaming individuals for performance issues?

- What is the downside of micromanagement?

- Name three key elements of process-first leadership.

Before delving into the next chapter, let's embark on a detailed exploration of SOP (Standard Operating Procedure) and SIPOC (Suppliers, Inputs, Process, Outputs, Customers). Understanding these two critical components is essential for achieving process excellence. This exploration will guide you through their definitions, design principles, and the profound impact they can have when integrated effectively.

By mastering SOPs and SIPOC, you'll gain valuable insights to enhance process efficiency and drive significant results. This foundational knowledge will serve as a navigational tool throughout the chapters ahead, empowering you to achieve deep, result-oriented benefits. Let's dive in and discover how these concepts can transform your approach to process management.

CHAPTER 3 A

Let's Understand SOP in detail (Standard Operating Procedures)

An SOP (Standard Operating Procedure) is a detailed, written instruction outlining the step by step journey to achieve consistent and efficient execution of tasks. It ensures quality and uniformity across processes.

FACTORS INVOLVED IN CREATING SOP:

- **Process Mapping:** Clearly define the step-by-step workflow and activities involved in the business process to create a comprehensive SOP.

- **Stakeholder Identification:** Identify all the relevant stakeholders, their requirements, and how they interact within the framework.

- **Performance Measurement:** Establish clear metrics and KPIs to track the effectiveness and efficiency of the SOP and SIPOC processes.

KEY COMPONENTS OF A SOP

1. **Purpose**

   - **Goal:**

     - Define the primary objectives of the SOP. What problem does it solve? What efficiency does it create? The goal should provide clarity on what the SOP aims to achieve, such as improving consistency, quality, or compliance.

- **Target Audience:**

  - Identify who will use the SOP. This could include employees at different levels, departments, or stakeholders involved in the process. Tailoring the content to their knowledge and skills can enhance understanding and effectiveness.

2. **Information**

   - **Data References:**

     - List any data or research that supports the procedures outlined in the SOP. This could include statistical data, previous case studies, or operational metrics demonstrating the need for the SOP.

   - **Sources:**

     - Identify where the information was sourced. This may include industry standards, regulatory guidelines, academic publications, or internal company documents. Citing credible sources can enhance the legitimacy of the SOP.

3. **Definition**

   - **Overview:**

     - Provide a concise description of what the SOP entails. This section should give a brief explanation of the processes covered, the context in which they operate, and any relevant terminology that will be used throughout the document.

   - **Importance:**

     - Explain why the SOP is crucial for the organization. Discuss potential risks of not following a standardized procedure, emphasizing how the SOP can enhance efficiency, safety, or compliance.

4. **Structure**

    - **Workflow:**

        - Present a clear sequence of steps in the SOP. A workflow diagram can be particularly useful here, outlining the process from start to finish and showing how different activities are interrelated.

    - **Visuals:**

        - Include any necessary charts, graphs, or images that can help clarify the SOP's content. Visual aids can enhance comprehension and retention, especially for complex processes.

5. **Scope**

    - **Inclusion:**

        - Specify what is included in the SOP. Outline the processes, departments, and functions that this SOP covers. This helps to provide a clear understanding of where the SOP applies.

    - **Exclusion:**

        - Clearly state what is not included in the SOP. This distinction helps avoid confusion and sets boundaries on the application of the SOP.

6. **Methodology**

    - **Step-By-Step Process:**

        - Provide detailed procedural steps in a clear, organized manner. Use bullet points or numbered lists to enhance readability. Each step should be actionable and concise, providing instructions that are easy to follow.

- **Decision Points:**

  - Identify critical decision-making junctures within the process. Explain what factors influence different choices and what actions should be taken depending on the outcomes of those decisions.

7. **Risk Marking**

   - **Risk Categorization:**

     - Identify and categorize various risks associated with the process. This could include operational, compliance, reputational, or financial risks. Classifying risks helps in better understanding and management.

   - **Mitigation Techniques:**

     - Offer strategies to mitigate identified risks. This may involve developing contingency plans, establishing checkpoints, or enhancing training requirements to ensure preparedness.

8. **Conclusion**

   - **Key Takeaways:**

     - Summarize the main points covered in the SOP. This helps reinforce important concepts and allows readers to quickly grasp the essential details.

   - **Importance Reiteration:**

     - Conclude by reiterating the importance of adhering to the SOP. Highlight its role in improving organizational efficiency, compliance, and quality.

9. **Approval Matrix**

   - **Stakeholder Approval:**

     - Define the necessary approval process for the SOP. List stakeholders or departments that must sign off before the

SOP is finalized and implemented, indicating their roles in the approval process.

- **Record Keeping:**

  - Specify how approvals will be documented and retained. Detail the documentation process to ensure transparency and accountability, which can assist in future audits or reviews.

10. **Control Mechanism**

- **Review Frequency:**

  - Identify how often the SOP should be reviewed and updated. Establishing a regular review cycle ensures that the SOP remains relevant and reflects any changes in processes or regulations.

- **Version Update:**

  - Outline the process for updating the SOP. Detail how changes will be communicated to stakeholders and how revisions will be documented, including the reasoning for changes and the new version number.

"Unlocking the Essential Advantages of Implementing Standard Operating Procedures (SOPs)"

1. **Consistency and Compliance:** Robust, well-structured SOPs ensures adherence by each team member, thereby reducing errors and ensuring regulatory compliance in all processes.

2. **Efficiency and Productivity:** With clearly defined SOPs, employee can perform tasks more efficiently, resulting in faster processing and reduced redundancies.

3. **Risk Mitigation:** The SOP helps in identify potential risks in the various processes, controls to mitigate these risks, safeguarding the institution against fraudulent activities and compliance violations.

4. **Training and Development:** The standardized procedures outlined in the SOPs can serve as a valuable training tool for new employees, facilitating their understanding of the process and ensuring consistency in service delivery.

5. **Improved Customer Experience:** With streamlined and standardized processes, any entity can enhance the overall customer experience by providing a smoother on boarding journey, reducing waiting time, and increasing customer satisfaction.

6. **Consistent Quality**: Ensure uniformity in deliverables, fostering trust and satisfaction among clients and stakeholders.

7. **Continuous Improvement**: Facilitate regular reviews and updates, promoting a culture of excellence and adaptability.

"Embrace SOPs for a more organized and effective organizational framework that drives success!"

CHAPTER 3 B

SIPOC – Definition and Purpose

SIPOC is a powerful tool used to map and analyze business processes. It stands for Suppliers, Inputs, Process, Outputs, and Customers - the key elements that define the scope and components of a process.

SIPOC Creation Process

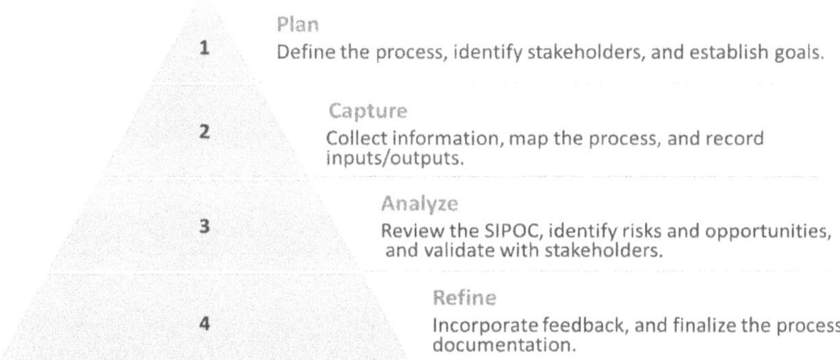

PROCESS MODELING FRAMEWORK

A systematic approach to map and analyze the steps in a business process. It helps identify inefficiencies, barriers, and opportunities for improvement.

Describe the Process: Clearly define the scope and objectives with starting and end point.

Identify Steps: Divide the process & define clearly into incremental steps.

Event Map: Use flowcharts or diagrams to visualize the process. Use custom symbols for actions, decisions, inputs, and outputs.

Explore the Event: Examine the system for inefficiencies & steps that do not add value.

Implement Changes: Based on the analysis, redesign the system to eliminate inefficiencies. Update the new policy and communicate the changes to all stakeholders.

Check and Repair: Continue to monitor the process to ensure the changes are effective. Make further adjustments as necessary to improve performance.

STAKE HOLDER ANALYSIS FRAMEWORK

Stakeholder analysis is a process of identifying and evaluating the influence and interests of various stakeholders in a project or business process.

Identifying stakeholders:

List all individuals / groups (internal / external) that have an interest or stake in the project.

Sort participants based on their location in the matrix:

High impact, high interest: Key stakeholders who need to be actively involved in decision making.

Low impact, high interest: Stakeholders should be informed and engaged as needed.

Low impact, low interest: Stakeholders will monitor with fewer interactions.

For each stakeholder group, make communication strategies based on their classification.

Get involved and connect: Implement strategies by engaging with stakeholders, addressing their concerns Monitoring and editing: Continually monitor stakeholder status and adjust communication.

SIPOC INTEGRATION WITH (SOPS)

Alignment:

Ensure that the SIPOC model aligns with and supports the organization's existing Standard Operating Procedures (SOPs). This integration creates a cohesive framework for operational efficiency and control.

Mapping:

Map the SIPOC components to the corresponding sections within the SOPs. This helps identify gaps, redundancies, and areas for streamlining to optimize the overall process.

Roles and Responsibilities

Clearly define the roles and responsibilities of each stakeholder involved in the SIPOC-SOP integration. This promotes accountability and ensures seamless execution of the defined processes.

SIPOC INTEGRATION TECHNIQUES

1 **Process Mapping**
Visualize the end-to-end flow

2 **Gap Analysis**
Identify areas for improvement

3 **Documentation**
Capture SIPOC details

4 **Automation**
Streamline SIPOC updates

Integrating SIPOC effectively requires a comprehensive approach. Begin by mapping out the entire process to visualize the flow. Next, conduct a gap analysis to identify areas for improvement. Thoroughly document the SIPOC details, and explore opportunities to automate the update process. These techniques will ensure the SIPOC remains a valuable tool for driving continuous optimization.

SIPOC diagrams are incredibly versatile and useful across various situations, especially when clarity and process mapping are key. Here are some common scenarios where they shine:

1. **Understanding Existing Processes**

   - When analysing current workflows to identify inefficiencies or bottlenecks.

   - Useful in industries like manufacturing or IT services to streamline operations.

2. **Initiating Process Improvement Projects**

   - Drive Lean, Six Sigma, or other methodologies

   - It provides a high-level overview before diving into detailed analysis.

3. **On boarding and Training**

   - Helps new employees quickly understand the critical components of a process.

   - Provides a clear visual for complex workflows, such as those in banking or healthcare.

4. **Cross-Functional Collaboration**

   - Aligns teams from different departments by clearly defining roles and contributions.

   - Ensures everyone understands the flow from suppliers to customers.

5. **Designing New Processes**

   - When launching new products, services, or systems.

   - Ensures all inputs, outputs, and stakeholders are accounted for.

6. **Auditing and Compliance**

   - Useful in regulated industries like pharmaceuticals or finance for documenting processes.

   - Simplifies internal and external audits by providing a structured overview.

7. **Customer Experience Enhancement**

   - Maps out the entire customer journey, ensuring inputs and outputs align with customer needs.

   - Particularly useful in retail, telecom, and IT industries.

8. **Problem-Solving**

   - When diagnosing where a process failure occurs (e.g., supplier issues or process inefficiencies).

   - Provides a logical framework for identifying root causes.

Here are some excellent tools for creating SIPOC diagrams:

1. **Lucid chart**: A versatile online diagramming tool that offers templates for SIPOC diagrams. It's user-friendly and great for collaboration.

2. **EdrawMax**: This tool provides a wide range of templates, including SIPOC diagrams, and allows for customization with colours, shapes, and icons.

3. **Microsoft Visio**: A professional diagramming tool that integrates well with other Microsoft Office applications. It's ideal for creating detailed SIPOC diagrams.

4. **Visual Paradigm**: Offers online SIPOC diagram templates and supports seamless collaboration. It's a good choice for teams working on process mapping.

5. **MyMap.AI**: An AI-powered SIPOC diagram maker that simplifies the process by generating diagrams based on your input.

6. **Canva**: While primarily a design tool, Canva can be used to create visually appealing SIPOC diagrams with its drag-and-drop interface.

7. **Smart Draw**: A powerful tool for creating various diagrams, including SIPOC, with pre-built templates and customization options.

Each of these tools has its strengths, so the best choice depends on your specific needs, such as collaboration, customization, or integration with other software.

LET'S TRY TO UNDERSTAND THE WHOLE CONCEPT OF SIPOC AT EACH LEVEL IN BANK`S LOAN PROCESSING

Suppliers

- **Customers:** Individuals or businesses applying for a loan.

- **Credit Bureaus:** Provide credit history and scores.

- **Internal Bank Departments:** Risk management, compliance, IT support.

- **External Auditors:** Ensure regulatory compliance.

- **Loan Officers:** Gather necessary documents and verify initial details.

Inputs

- **Loan Application Forms:** Details provided by customers.

- **Customer Financial Data:** Income, expenses, and other financial details.

- **Credit Scores:** Data from credit bureaus.

- **Collateral Information:** Details of collateral provided for secured loans.

- **KYC Documents:** Identity verification documents.

- **Bank Policy Guidelines:** Internal guidelines for loan approval.

- **Regulatory Requirements:** Compliance-related documentation.

Process

1. **Loan Application Submission:** Customer submits the loan application with necessary documents.

2. **Initial Verification:** Loan officer verifies the completeness of the application and documents.

3. **Credit Assessment:** Credit team evaluates the customer's creditworthiness.

4. **Risk Analysis:** Risk management team assesses potential risks associated with the loan.

5. **Collateral Valuation:** For secured loans, the collateral is valued.

6. **Compliance Check:** The compliance team ensures all regulatory requirements are met.

7. **Loan Approval/Rejection:** Based on the analysis, the loan is either approved or rejected.

8. **Loan Agreement:** If approved, a loan agreement is created and signed by both parties.

9. **Disbursement:** Loan amount is disbursed to the customer's account.

10. **Post-Disbursement Monitoring:** Regular monitoring of loan repayments and compliance with terms.

11. **Agency reporting:** Disbursement data reporting to Bureau and collateral to CERSAI.

Outputs

- **Approved/Rejected Loan Application:** Outcome of the loan application process.

- **Loan Agreement:** Contract between the bank and the customer.

- **Disbursement Report:** Record of the loan amount disbursed.

- **Compliance Report:** Documentation ensuring regulatory adherence.

- **Customer Feedback:** Feedback collected from customers regarding the process.

Customers

- **Loan Applicants:** Individuals or businesses receiving the loan.

- **Bank Management:** Internal stakeholders monitoring the loan portfolio.

- **Regulatory Authorities:** Entities overseeing compliance with financial regulations.

- **Credit Bureaus:** Receive updates on the loan's status and repayment.

- **Internal Audit Team:** Reviews the process to ensure adherence to policies and regulations.

Risk / Challenge(s) identification at each step of entire process of Loan Processing

Step 1: Loan Application Submission

Supplier: Customer

Input: Loan Application, KYC Docs, Financial Data

Output: Loan application logged into the system

Challenges: Incomplete documentation leads to delays.

Step 2: Initial Verification

Supplier: Loan Officer

Input: Loan Application, KYC Documents

Output: Verified application ready for credit check

Challenges: Manual verification is prone to human error and time consuming too.

Step 3: Credit Assessment

Supplier: Credit Bureau, Internal Credit Team

Input: Credit Score, Financial Data

Output: Credit report with risk assessment

Challenges: Inconsistent scoring models can lead to inaccurate risk assessment.

Step 4: Risk Analysis

Supplier: Risk Management Team

Input: Credit Assessment, Collateral Information

Output: Risk report

Challenges: Complex Risk can delay the process

Step 5: Compliance Check

Supplier: Compliance Department

Input: Regulatory requirements

Output: Compliance report

Challenges: Regulatory requirements can change frequently, requiring constant updates to processes.

Step 6: Loan Approval/Rejection

Supplier: Credit Committee

Input: Risk Report, Compliance Report

Output: Approved/Rejected Application

Challenges: Approval process can be slow, especially for high-value loans.

Step 7: Loan Agreement

Supplier: Legal Team

Input: Approved Application

Output: Loan Agreement

Challenges: Legal documentation can be complex and time-consuming to prepare.

Step 8: Disbursement

Supplier: Finance Department

Input: Signed Loan Agreement

Output: Disbursed Loan Amount

Challenges: Delays in disbursement due to bank processing times.

Step 9: Post-Disbursement Monitoring

Supplier: Loan Monitoring Team

Input: Disbursed Loan Details, Repayment Schedule

Output: Monitoring Reports

Challenges: Ensuring timely repayments and detecting early signs of default.

Key Findings

Manual Processes: Several steps were heavily reliant on manual intervention, leading to delays and errors.

Compliance Delays: Frequent changes in regulations were not promptly communicated, causing bottlenecks.

Inconsistent Risk Assessment: Variability in risk assessment methods across different departments.

Proposed Improvements

1. Automation of Verification Process: Implement an automated document verification system to reduce manual errors.

2. Integrated Credit Scoring Model: Develop a consistent credit scoring model to be used across all departments.

3. Regulatory Updates Dashboard: compliance team to create a real-time dashboard to stay updated on regulatory changes.

4. Workflow Optimization: Redesign the loan approval workflow for better TAT & reducing overall processing time.

FINAL THOUGHTS

Adoption of SIPOC methodology helped entity in visualizing the entire Loan Origination Process, identifying critical pain points, and carrying out targeted enhancements. In turn, this resulted significant decrease in processing time, increased consumer satisfaction, and improved compliance with regulatory requirements. The entity was able to more easily streamline operations and accomplish its objectives as a result of the clear and concise SIPOC diagram.

CONCLUSION AND TAKEAWAYS

In this comprehensive case study, we have explored the power of SIPOC in improving financial processes. From defining the key components to creating detailed flowcharts and mitigating risks, SIPOC has emerged as a versatile tool for driving operational excellence.

CHAPTER 4

Mapping Your Way to Efficiency: The Process Mapping Guide

INTRODUCTION

Many businesses operate in a state of "organized chaos." Employees know what to do, but the overall workflow remains unclear, undocumented, and inefficient. This chapter introduces process mapping, a powerful technique to transform this chaos into clarity, creating a visual roadmap for improved efficiency, scalability, and growth.

SECTION 1: THE HIDDEN COSTS OF "INVISIBLE" PROCESSES

1.1. The Problem with Tribal Knowledge

Many businesses rely on "tribal knowledge"—an informal understanding of processes held by only a few key individuals. This creates significant vulnerabilities.

→ **Employee Turnover:** Losing key personnel leads to knowledge loss and process disruption.

→ **On boarding Challenges:** New hires struggle to understand undocumented workflows, leading to inefficiencies and errors.

→ **Inconsistent Customer Experiences:** Variability in processes leads to inconsistencies in service quality, negatively impacting customer satisfaction.

1.2. Case Study: The Unmapped E-commerce Startup

A rapidly growing e-commerce Startup initially managed supplier orders manually. This worked until they scaled. When new employees joined, they lacked clear guidance, resulting in delays, lost orders, and angry customers.

→ **The Solution:** Mapping out their supply chain revealed bottlenecks and inefficiencies. Automating key steps and documenting the workflow dramatically reduced order errors (by 70%).

→ **The Lesson:** You can't improve what you can't see. Process mapping is the first step toward optimizing any business process.

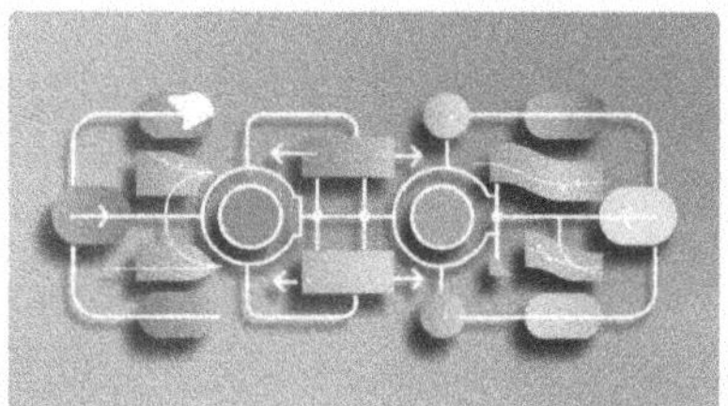

SECTION 2: THE SIMPLE PROCESS MAPPING FORMULA

2.1. A Practical, Jargon-Free Approach

This section presents a straightforward, five-step process mapping formula, eliminating unnecessary jargon and focusing on practical application.

→ **Step 1: Identify the Process:** Clearly define the process you want to map.

→ **Step 2: Define Start and End Points:** Establish clear boundaries for the process.

→ **Step 3: List Key Steps:** Describe each step concisely, including who performs the action.

→ **Step 4: Visualize the Process:** Use flowcharts, swim lane diagrams, or even sticky notes to create a visual representation.

→ **Step 5: Identify Inefficiencies:** Analyse the map to identify bottlenecks, redundancies, and areas for improvement.

2.2. Case Study: The Pizza Shop Process Map

A local pizzeria experienced frequent order delays. By mapping out their process (customer order, kitchen preparation, packing & delivery), they identified a bottleneck at order entry. Implementing a digital POS system drastically improved order fulfilment speed (by 40%).

Pizza Shop Workflow

1   Order
   Customer places order

2   Prep
   Dough prepared, toppings added

3   Bake
   Pizza cooked in oven

4   Serve
   Delivered to customer

SECTION 3: FROM MESS TO MASTERY: A FICTIONAL CASE STUDY

3.1. The XYZ Logistics Challenge: A Story of Transformation

This section introduces a fictional case study, "From Mess to Mastery," following the journey of XYZ Logistics as they transformed their operations using process mapping.

- **The Initial Situation:** XYZ Logistics was experiencing rapid growth but suffered from massive inefficiencies. Problems included lost shipments, frustrated employees, and soaring customer complaints.

- **Raj's Insight:** Raj, the operations manager, realized that the key was to map the entire workflow and visualize the bottlenecks.

- **The Transformation:** Using the process mapping formula, Raj identified key issues: too many manual approvals, duplicate data entry, and a lack of real-time shipment tracking. He implemented solutions: automated order tracking, standardized forms, and elimination of unnecessary approvals.

3.2. The Results: XYZ Logistics experienced a 50% increase in efficiency, improved employee morale, and significantly enhanced customer satisfaction.

SECTION 4: AVOIDING COMMON MISTAKES IN PROCESS MAPPING

- **Over complication:** Keep it simple and visual.

- **Technology First:** Fix the process before automating.

- **Lack of Review and Updating:** Processes evolve, so regular reviews are essential.

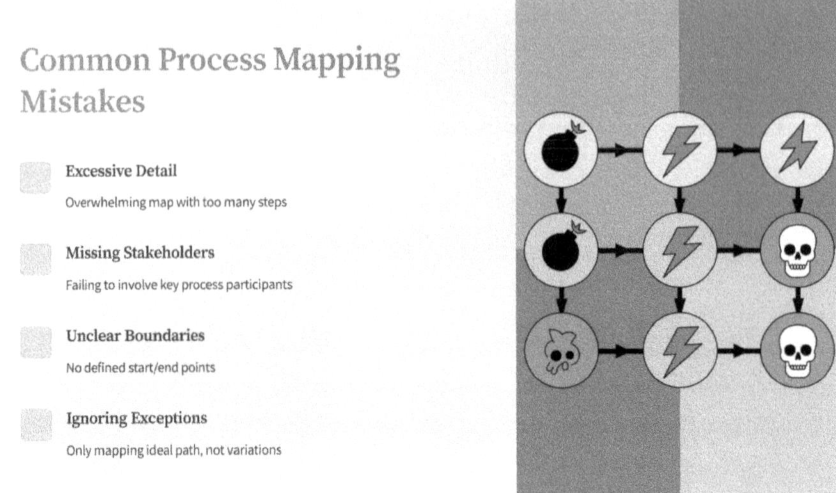

SECTION 5: THE POWER OF A WELL-MAPPED PROCESS

- Predictable, scalable workflows.

- Easier training for new hires.

- Improved efficiency and customer experience.

Concluding Statement & Final Thought

Process mapping is not just a technique; it's a fundamental shift in mindset. By visualizing your workflows, you gain the clarity and insights necessary to identify inefficiencies, streamline processes, and ultimately drive sustainable growth. Remember: "You can't optimize what you don't understand. Map it, simplify it, and scale it!"

Let us summarize and understand the chapter through a beautiful story

The Speedy Spoon: A Restaurant Revolution

"The Speedy Spoon" was a popular local restaurant known for its delicious food, but they suffered from long wait times and inconsistent service. Their owner, Carlos, a talented chef, was struggling to keep up with demand. His restaurant felt chaotic, despite the kitchen's efficiency. He needed better processes.

A management consultant, Maria, recommended using SIPOC to map their service process. This is what they mapped:

→ **Suppliers:** Food suppliers, kitchen staff, wait staff, reservation system, cleaning crew.

→ **Inputs:** Food ingredients, kitchen equipment, tables, menus, staff schedules, customer orders.

→ **Process:** (This is where they would define their SOPs, for tasks like order taking, food preparation, delivery, customer interaction, billing, etc.)

- Customer greeting and seating.

- Order taking (accurate recording).

- Food preparation (following recipes exactly).

- Food delivery (timely and correct).

- Bill processing and payment.

- Customer feedback collection.

→ **Outputs:** Satisfied customers, sales data, customer feedback, waste, staff performance data.

→ **Customers:** Diners, delivery services.

By implementing detailed SOPs for each stage and using SIPOC for oversight:

→ **Reduced Wait Times:** Streamlined order-taking and food delivery procedures significantly improved service speed.

→ **Improved Consistency:** Standardized recipes and service protocols ensured consistent food quality and customer service.

→ **Enhanced Teamwork:** Clear roles and responsibilities improved coordination among staff members.

→ **Increased Efficiency:** Optimized workflows reduced waste and improved resource utilization.

The Speedy Spoon became a model of efficiency and customer satisfaction. Carlos, having embraced process mastery, could focus on creating new menu items and expanding his business.

Quote: *"What you don't map, you can't master. Clarity is the first step to control."*

Puzzle:

- **Process Mapping Challenge:** Think of a simple daily task (making coffee, sending an email). List the key steps involved.

Quiz:

- What is "tribal knowledge," and why is it a problem?

- List the five steps of the process mapping formula.

- What are some common mistakes to avoid while process mapping?

CHAPTER 5

The 3-Step Efficiency Formula: Automate, Delegate, Eliminate

INTRODUCTION

In today's competitive landscape, efficiency isn't just desirable—it's essential for survival and growth. This chapter introduces a powerful three-step formula—Automate, Delegate, eliminate—to help you identify and eliminate inefficiencies, freeing up valuable time and resources to focus on what truly matters: strategic growth and innovation.

SECTION 1: THE 80/20 RULE: IDENTIFYING THE HIGH-IMPACT 20%

1.1. The Pareto Principle in Action

This principle reveals a fundamental truth about business inefficiencies: 80% of problems stem from just 20% of the underlying issues. By identifying and addressing this critical 20%, you can achieve dramatic improvements in efficiency.

1.2. Common Sources of Inefficiency

Redundant, manual, and outdated processes are major contributors to inefficiency.

→ **Redundant Processes:** Duplicate tasks or steps that add no value.

→ **Manual Processes:** Repetitive tasks that could be automated.

→ **Outdated Processes:** Processes that are no longer relevant or efficient.

1.3. Case Study: Manual Data Entry

A company spent countless hours manually entering customer data—a task easily automated using an AI-powered CRM. This highlights how identifying inefficient processes is the first step towards improving efficiency.

Manual vs. Automated Data Entry

Manual Entry	Automated Entry
Time-consuming	Fast processing
Error-prone	High accuracy
Labor-intensive	Resource efficient

SECTION 2: STEP 1: AUTOMATE – LEVERAGING TECHNOLOGY FOR EFFICIENCY

2.1. The Power of Automation

It is the key to eliminating repetitive and predictable tasks, freeing up human capital for more strategic and creative endeavours. Technology handles tasks better and faster than humans can.

2.2. Checklist for Automation

- **Repetitive Manual Tasks:** Data entry, report generation, email responses.

- **Zero-Creativity Tasks:** Process require minimal or no independent judgment.

- **Structured Data Tasks:** Financial processing, invoice generation, CRM data management.

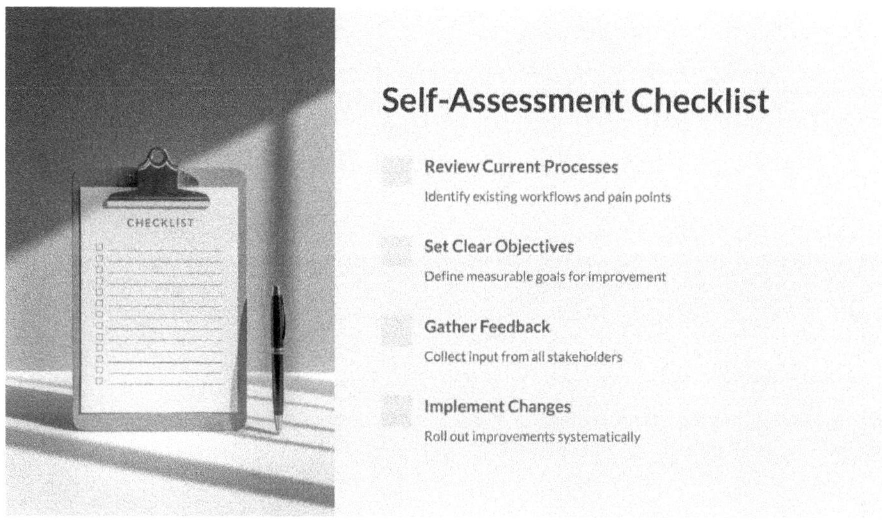

2.3. Real-World Examples

- **AI Chabot's in Customer Service:** Providing instant support and resolving common queries, freeing up human agents for more complex issues.

2.4. Actionable Tips for Automation

- Experiment with tools like Zapier, UiPath, or Microsoft Power Automate. Start small and gradually expand automation across your operations.

SECTION 3: STEP 2: DELEGATE – OPTIMIZING YOUR TIME AND RESOURCES

3.1. The Power of Delegation

Delegation involves assigning tasks that require human input but do not necessarily demand your specific expertise. This frees you to concentrate on your core strengths and strategic priorities.

3.2. Checklist for Delegation

- **Non-Core Tasks:** Activities outside your area of expertise.

→ **Time-Consuming Recurring Tasks:** Tasks that take more than 10 hours a week.

→ **Cost-Effective Outsourcing:** Tasks that can be performed more cost-effectively by external resources.

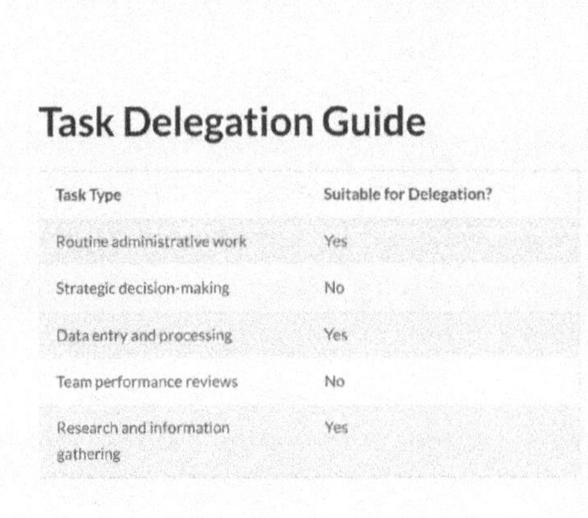

Task Delegation Guide

Task Type	Suitable for Delegation?
Routine administrative work	Yes
Strategic decision-making	No
Data entry and processing	Yes
Team performance reviews	No
Research and information gathering	Yes

3.3. Real-World Examples: Effective Delegation

- **Entrepreneurs and VAs:** CEOs outsourcing administrative tasks to VAs (Virtual Assistants).

- **Google's Outsourcing Strategy:** Outsourcing non-core functions to specialized vendors.

3.4. Actionable Tips for Delegation

- Use freelance platforms (Upwork, Fiverr) or virtual assistant services. Clearly define roles, responsibilities, and expectations.

SECTION 4: STEP 3: ELIMINATE – REMOVING DEAD WEIGHT

4.1. Ruthlessly Removing Non-Essential Tasks

The elimination step involves identifying and removing tasks that add no measurable value to your business. This requires a ruthless assessment of your processes, eliminating unnecessary activities.

4.2. Checklist for Elimination

- **Unused Reports:** Reports that are never reviewed or acted upon.

- **Unnecessary Approvals:** Excessive approval layers slowing down decision-making.

- **Redundant Meetings:** Meetings that could be replaced by emails or shorter sessions.

- **Outdated Processes:** Processes that are no longer needed.

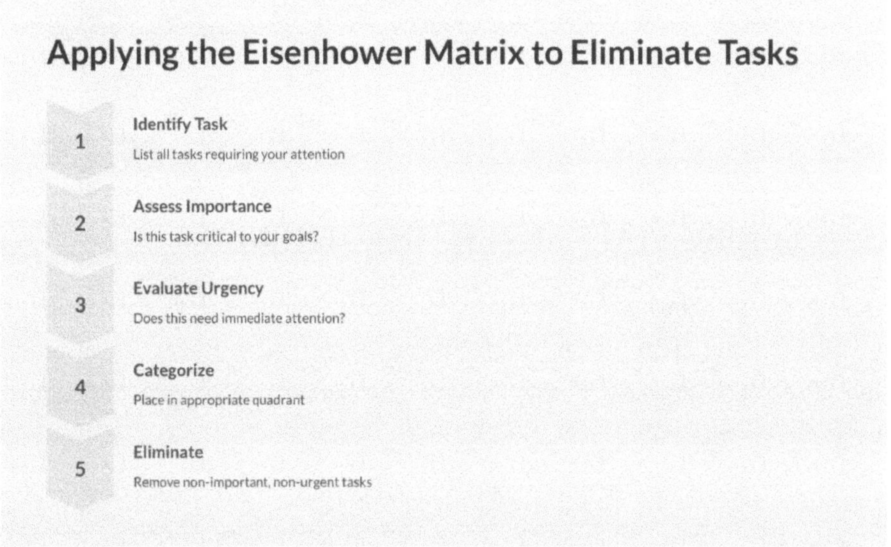

4.4. Actionable Tip: The Eisenhower Matrix

Use the Eisenhower Matrix (Urgent/Important) to prioritize tasks and identify those that can be eliminated.

SECTION 5: THE A.D.E. AUDIT: A QUICK SELF-DIAGNOSIS

This section provides a step-by-step guide to help readers analyse their processes using the Automate, Delegate, Eliminate framework.

- → **Step 1:** List all daily/weekly tasks.

- → **Step 2:** Categorize each task (Automate, Delegate, Eliminate).

→ **Step 3:** Implement one change per week and measure the impact.

The A.D.E. Audit Guide

A - Assess — Evaluate current state and identify gaps

D - Develop — Create action plans to address findings

E - Execute — Implement solutions and measure results

CONCLUDING STATEMENT & FINAL THOUGHT

Mastering the Automate, Delegate, eliminate framework is essential for creating a truly efficient and scalable business. Companies that embrace this three-step approach will achieve greater speed, lower costs, and increased profitability.

The Case of the Missing Millions (Banking), This story powerfully illustrates the financial impact of inefficient processes and the benefits of automation, delegation, and elimination. The community bank's transformation from unexplained financial losses to financial stability and improved efficiency serves as a compelling example of how this three-step framework can solve real-world problems and lead to remarkable improvements.

Let us summarize and understand the chapter through a beautiful story

Banking: The Case of the Missing Millions

Once upon a time, in the quaint town of Willow Creek, nestled amidst rolling hills, stood "Friendly Finances," a small community bank known for its personalized service. However, Friendly Finances faced a growing problem: unexplained discrepancies in their financial records. Small amounts went missing, and while not individually catastrophic, they added up, creating significant losses over time. The bank's owner, a kind but overwhelmed woman named Martha, knew she needed help but didn't know where to start.

Enter David, a seasoned process consultant. He introduced Martha to the power of Standard Operating Procedures (SOPs) and SIPOC analysis. David explained that SOPs were detailed, step-by-step instructions for every process, while SIPOC provided a framework to understand the whole system.

Let's focus on the "Internal Fund Transfers" process. The SIPOC analysis revealed the following:

→ **Suppliers:** Teller staff, internal accounting department, online banking system.

→ **Inputs:** Customer requests, transfer amounts, account details, security authorizations.

→ **Process:** (This is where the detailed SOPs would come in, with steps like: Receive transfer request, verify account details, authorize transaction, update records, generate confirmation, etc.)

→ **Outputs:** Successful fund transfers, transaction records, audit trails, error reports.

→ **Customers:** Internal departments, customers making transfers.

David and Martha created detailed SOPs for every stage of internal fund transfers. Each step was precisely defined, including security protocols and error-handling procedures. This enhanced control and transparency, and the SIPOC analysis revealed a critical weakness: the lack of mandatory double-checking for large transactions. A simple, automated alert system was added to the SOP, flagging large transfers for additional verification.

Implementing SOPs and SIPOC at Friendly Finances resulted in:

→ **Elimination of errors:** The detailed steps reduced human error, which was a major source of the missing funds.

→ **Improved accuracy:** Mandatory double-checking for large transfers greatly reduced errors.

→ **Increased efficiency:** Streamlined processes saved time and resources.

→ **Enhanced compliance:** The system was more auditable, meeting regulatory requirements.

With the new SOPs and insights from the SIPOC analysis, Friendly Finances transformed from a bank with unexplained losses to a financially sound and reliable institution. Martha, no longer overwhelmed, could focus on expanding the business and providing exceptional customer service.

Quote: *"Efficiency isn't doing more with less—it's doing less of what doesn't matter."*

Puzzle:

- **ADE Scenario:** You spend 10 hours a week creating social media posts. Is this a task you should Automate, Delegate, or Eliminate? Why?

Quiz:

→ List the three steps of the efficiency formula.

→ Give an example of a task that is a good candidate for automation.

CHAPTER 6

The Pareto Principle: Unlocking Efficiency by Focusing on What Matters Most

INTRODUCTION

Most businesses waste valuable time and resources tackling minor issues while ignoring the critical few that drive the majority of results. In the previous chapter, as you touched upon the concept of the Pareto Principle, this chapter will now take a deeper dive into its details. This chapter introduces the Principle (80/20 rule), a powerful framework for identifying and prioritizing the 20% of efforts that yield 80% of the results, unlocking significant improvements in efficiency and productivity.

SECTION 1: UNDERSTANDING THE 80/20 RULE

1.1. The Core Concept: The Power of the Vital Few

The Principle reveals a fundamental truth about business: A small percentage of factors often accounts for a disproportionately large share of the outcomes. In process management, this means that 80% of inefficiencies often stem from just 20% of broken processes.

1.2. The Cost of Misdirected Effort

Businesses frequently waste time and resources trying to optimize everything, instead of focusing on the critical 20% that drives the most significant results. A McKinsey study reveals that businesses waste up to 30% of their time on low-value tasks that don't contribute to growth.

1.3. Avoiding the Common Pitfalls:

Avoid these common mistakes:

→ **Over-optimizing:** Trying to optimize everything instead of focusing on the most impactful areas.

→ **Ignoring the Vital Few:** Neglecting to address the 20% of critical issues that account for 80% of problems.

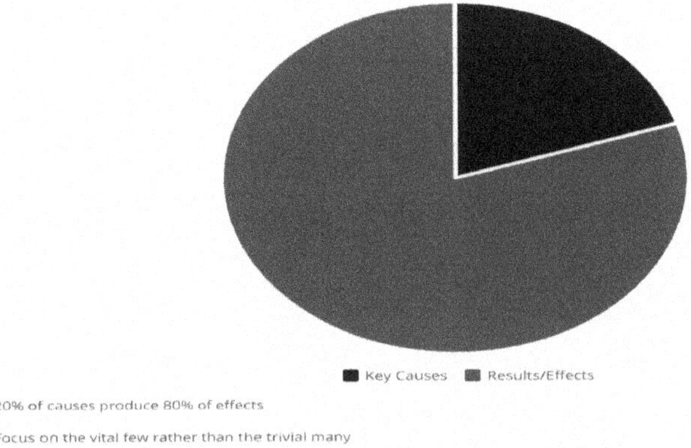

SECTION 2: IDENTIFYING THE HIGH-IMPACT 20%

2.1. Not All Inefficiencies Are Created Equal

The Principle highlights that not all inefficiencies are equal. Some have a disproportionate impact on overall results. Identifying these high-impact areas is the key to maximizing your efforts.

2.2. Checklist for Identifying the High-Impact 20%

Use this checklist to analyse your processes:

→ **Customer Complaints and Delays:** What causes the most customer dissatisfaction or delays?

→ **Revenue and Customer Satisfaction:** Which processes directly impact revenue and customer satisfaction?

→ **Resource Consumption:** Which tasks consume the most time and resources but offer minimal impact?

Sample Checklist

Process Analysis Checklist

1. **Define the Process**

   - What is the objective of the process?

   - What are the key outputs and outcomes expected?

2. **Map the Process**

   - Have you documented each step in the process?

   - Are all roles and responsibilities clearly outlined?

3. **Identify Inputs and Resources**

   - What inputs are required for the process (materials, information, etc.)?

   - Are resources (human, technological, financial) adequately allocated?

4. **Analyse Process Performance**

   - What metrics are currently used to measure performance?

   - Are these metrics aligned with business goals?

   - Have you collected data on process efficiency and effectiveness?

5. **Identify Bottlenecks and Inefficiencies**

   - Are there steps in the process that cause delays?

   - Have you identified any redundancies or unnecessary steps?

   - Is the process consistent, or does it vary significantly?

6. **Assess Compliance and Risk Management**

    - Does the process adhere to relevant regulations and standards?

    - Have you identified any risks associated with the process?

    - Are there controls in place to mitigate identified risks?

7. **Gather Feedback**

    - Have you sought input from employees involved in the process?

    - Are customers or stakeholders consulted about their needs and expectations?

8. **Evaluate Technology Utilization**

    - Is technology being used effectively in the process?

    - Are there opportunities to automate or enhance with new technology?

9. **Identify Improvement Opportunities**

    - What changes could be made to enhance efficiency or quality?

    - Are there best practices from other industries that could be integrated?

10. **Develop an Action Plan**

    - Have you prioritized improvement opportunities based on impact?

    - Is there a clear plan for implementing changes, including timelines and responsibilities?

    - How will you monitor and evaluate the effectiveness of these changes?

CONCLUSION

- Have you scheduled regular reviews of the process to ensure continuous improvement?

- Will you be sharing the findings and improvements with relevant stakeholders?

SECTION 3: APPLYING THE PRINCIPLE TO WORKFLOW OPTIMIZATION

3.1. The 80/20 Rule in Action:

Many businesses spend 80% of their time firefighting low-impact problems while neglecting the root causes. This reactive approach prevents efficient problem-solving and sustained growth.

3.2. Common Traps to Avoid

- **Over-analysing minor issues:** Spending too much time on low-impact problems.

- **Investing in technology without fixing broken workflows:** Technology is a tool, not a solution. Fix your processes before investing in new technology.

- **Fixing things that aren't broken:** This wastes time and resources.

3.3. Actionable Tip: Conducting a Process Bottleneck Audit

Perform a process bottleneck audit to identify the 20% of inefficiencies responsible for 80% of your delays.

SECTION 4: APPLYING THE PRINCIPLE TO DIFFERENT BUSINESS AREAS

- **Sales & Marketing:** Focus on high-value customers and top-performing channels.

- **Operations & Efficiency:** Target the major bottlenecks and sources of errors.

- **Customer Service:** Address recurring issues and streamline support processes.

SECTION 5: THE FIX-IT FRAMEWORK: A 3-STEP PROCESS AUDIT

- **Step 1:** Identify key processes and pain points.

- **Step 2:** Find the 20% of inefficiencies causing 80% of problems.

- **Step 3:** Prioritize fixing these critical issues.

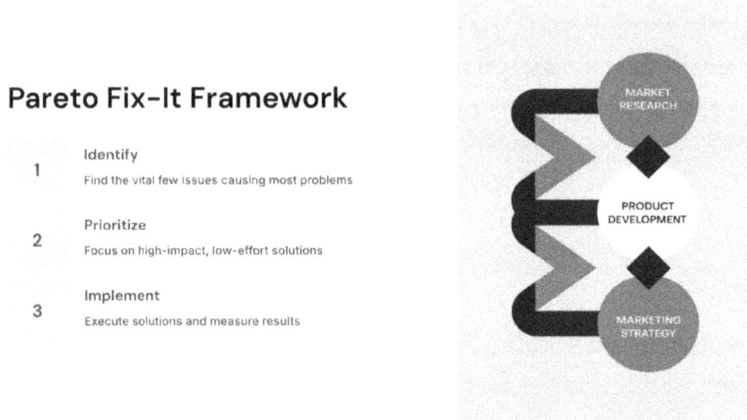

SECTION 6: CASE STUDY: IPHONE SUPPLY CHAIN MASTERY

Apple streamlined its supply chain by concentrating on the top suppliers, leading to faster production cycles, enhanced quality, and greater operational efficiency. This strategic focus exemplifies supply chain excellence. The supplier optimization approach serves as a strong real-world application of this Principle.

Final Thought

This Principle is a powerful tool for achieving significant improvements in efficiency and productivity. By focusing on the vital 20%, businesses can achieve 80% of their desired results. Remember, process mastery is about working smarter, not harder.

Let us summarize and understand the chapter through a beautiful story

The Seamless Dance of Efficiency in a Modern Coffeehouse

In the bustling heart of a quaint but rapidly growing city, the aroma of fresh-brewed coffee wafted through the air as Morning Brew, a beloved local coffee shop, buzzed with its usual morning frenzy. However, beneath the comforting ambiance of this cherished caffeine haven lay a tale of efficiency unlocked by the strategic embrace of the SIPOC, SOP methods, and the Pareto Principle.

Morning Brew was known for its artisanal brews and exquisite pastries, consistently attracting a diverse crowd of both locals and tourists. Yet, beneath the surface, the shop faced challenges. Lengthy order times and occasional shortages marred customer experience, making efficiency the need of the hour.

Identifying the High-Impact 20% – A SIPOC Analysis:

Realizing the need for change, the shop owners decided to audit their processes using the SIPOC method. By mapping out Suppliers, Inputs, Processes, Outputs, and Customers, they identified critical bottlenecks: the coffee bean delivery delays and the complex order-taking process that led to errors.

Optimizing with the Pareto Principle:

Empowered by the Principle, the team at Morning Brew shifted focus. Instead of superficially addressing every complaint, they zeroed in on the "vital few" processes causing the majority of issues. With customer feedback indicating that 80% of complaints stemmed from just 20% of their operational processes, the owners had clear direction.

Implementing SOP for Impactful Change:

A streamlined Standard Operating Procedure (SOP) for order-taking was devised. Order takers were trained to use a tactile, user-friendly tablet interface, reducing human error and increasing order accuracy. Simultaneously, they focused on strengthening relationships with a select group of top coffee bean suppliers to ensure timely deliveries and maintain superior quality.

The Result: A Symphony of Efficiency and Satisfaction

The transformation was remarkable. Order processing times dropped dramatically, with customer satisfaction ratings soaring to unprecedented heights. Bottlenecks were unclogged, allowing the energetic hum of Morning Brew to unify into a seamless ballet of skilled coffee makers and patrons, each interaction refined to perfection.

CONCLUSION

Through their application of the Pareto Principle, SIPOC, and SOP, Morning Brew epitomized process mastery. By homing in on the pivotal processes that held the greatest sway over their operations, they generated a profound improvement in efficiency and customer experience. Their story serves as an illustration of unlocking potential by focusing on what truly matters—the vital few that drive the greatest impact.

The Morning Brew's voyage from chaos to order teaches a lesson invaluable across all industries: It's not about doing more, but about doing what truly counts.

Quote: *"The secret to scaling isn't in fixing everything—it's in fixing what matters most."*

Quiz:

- What is the core concept of the Pareto Principle?
- What are some common traps to avoid when applying the Pareto Principle?
- What are the three steps of the Fix-It Framework?

CHAPTER 7

Silent Profit Killers: Identifying and Sealing Hidden Process Leaks

INTRODUCTION

Many businesses celebrate revenue growth, often overlooking the subtle yet significant drain of "silent profit killers"—small inefficiencies that compound into major financial losses over time. These hidden leaks often stem from operational, financial, or compliance issues, all of which are significantly impacted by a lack of well-defined Standard Operating Procedures (SOPs) and a failure to fully utilize the power of SIPOC (Suppliers, Inputs, Process, Outputs, Customers) analysis. This chapter will equip you to identify these hidden leaks and implement effective strategies to mitigate them, maximizing your profitability.

SECTION 1: THE HIGH COST OF SEEMINGLY SMALL MISTAKES

1.1. The Hidden Drain: Unveiling the True Cost of Inefficiency

Studies reveal that businesses lose a considerable 5-10% of their annual revenue due to process inefficiencies, fraud, and non-compliance. These aren't catastrophic failures; instead, they are small, seemingly insignificant errors that compound into substantial losses over time.

1.2. The Key to Profit Protection: A Proactive Approach

Process optimization is not just about growing revenue; it's about safeguarding the profits you've already earned. This requires a proactive approach to identify and eliminate hidden process leaks. This chapter outlines the steps to achieving this, leveraging the power of SOPs and SIPOC analysis.

SECTION 2: OPERATIONAL RISKS: IDENTIFYING AND ADDRESSING INEFFICIENCIES

2.1. Understanding Operational Process Leaks

This section identifies common operational issues that lead to delays, errors, and lost revenue.

2.2. Common Operational Process Leaks and their Impact

- **Redundant Approvals:** Excessive layers of approval significantly slow decision-making, causing delays and frustration.

- **Lack of Standard Operating Procedures (SOPs):** Inconsistent procedures lead to errors, inconsistent results, and reduced efficiency. Detailed SOPs create a clear roadmap for every task, minimizing ambiguity and ensuring consistent performance.

- **Data Entry Errors:** Inaccurate data entry contributes to incorrect billing, payroll errors, order mismatches, and other costly mistakes.

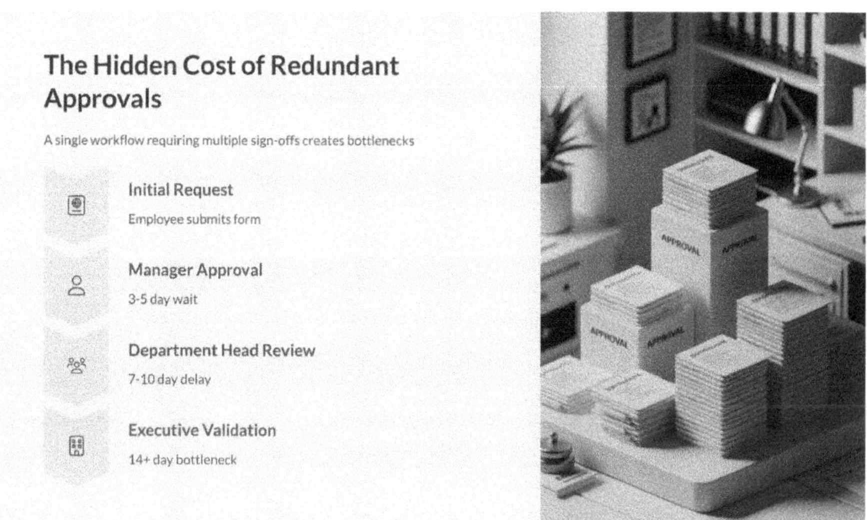

SECTION 3: FINANCIAL RISKS: THE SILENT MONEY DRAINS

3.1. Unnoticed Financial Inefficiencies: The Hidden Costs

Unnoticed financial inefficiencies represent a significant drain on profits. This section examines common financial process leaks.

3.2. Common Financial Process Leaks

- **Unclaimed Vendor Discounts:** Failure to track vendor discounts leads to lost savings.

- **Hidden Fees:** Overlooked fees in banking transactions and other areas erode profits.

- **Revenue Leakage:** Inaccurate pricing or discounting practices can lead to significant revenue loss.

- **Cash Flow Mismanagement:** Poor cash flow management can lead to liquidity crises.

3.3. Case Study: Target's Data Breach Incident (2013)

Overview: In 2013, Target Corporation faced a significant data breach compromising personal and financial information of approximately 40 million customers, revealing vulnerabilities in its data security systems.

Challenges Identified

1. **Insufficient Cybersecurity Measures:** Weak security protocols allowed hackers access to sensitive customer data.

2. **Delayed Response to Alerts:** Anomalies were detected but not addressed promptly, prolonging customer data exposure.

3. **Lack of Comprehensive Vendor Management:** The breach originated from a third-party vendor's compromised credentials, highlighting weaknesses in managing external partners.

   Target's Response: To mitigate risks and enhance security, Target implemented several measures:

Actionable Lessons

1. **Conduct Thorough Risk Assessments:**

   Strategy: Regularly evaluate security protocols to identify vulnerabilities.

   Application: Perform audits to proactively address potential risks.

2. **Improve Incident Response Plans:**

   Strategy: Develop effective plans and communication protocols for addressing security breaches.

   Application: Update incident response procedures and train employees accordingly.

3. **Strengthen Vendor Management Practices:**

   Strategy: Implement stricter security requirements for third-party vendors.

Application: Conduct thorough assessments to ensure compliance with security standards.

Info source: https://redriver.com/security/target-data-breach

SECTION 4: COMPLIANCE RISKS: AVOIDING COSTLY LEGAL LANDMINES

4.1. Regulatory Oversights: The High Cost of Non-Compliance

Non-compliance with regulations leads to significant penalties and reputational damage. This section highlights the importance of establishing robust compliance processes.

4.2. Common Compliance Process Leaks

- **Inconsistent KYC/AML Checks:** Leading to regulatory fines.

- **Incorrect Tax Filings:** Resulting in financial penalties.

- **GDPR & Data Privacy Violations:** Exposing sensitive customer information can lead to substantial fines and reputational harm.

- **Untracked Employee Labour Laws:** Non-compliance with labour laws leads to lawsuits and damage to company reputation.

4.3. Case Study: Wells Fargo Fake Account Scandal (2016)

Wells Fargo's fake account scandal demonstrates the devastating consequences of ignoring compliance. Employees created fake customer accounts to meet targets, leading to billions of dollars in penalties and irreparable reputational damage.

> → **SIPOC Analysis:** A well-defined SIPOC analysis of the account opening process would have highlighted the vulnerabilities within the existing system. Identifying all Suppliers (technology providers, compliance teams), Inputs (customer data, application forms), the Process (account application, verification, opening), Outputs

(new accounts, compliance data), and Customers (account holders) would have allowed for a more robust system design.

→ **Robust SOPs:** Clear SOPs, outlining the steps for opening accounts, verifying customer information, ensuring compliance with regulations, and implementing strong internal controls, would have prevented this scandal.

Info source: https://en.wikipedia.org/wiki/Wells_Fargo_cross-selling_scandal

SECTION 5: THE PROFIT LEAK AUDIT: A PRACTICAL SELF-ASSESSMENT

This section provides a step-by-step guide for conducting a profit leak audit to identify and address potential risks.

→ **Step 1:** List your top five business processes.

→ **Step 2:** For each process, identify potential operational, financial, and compliance risks.

→ **Step 3:** Implement automation, process improvements, or monitoring systems to mitigate these risks.

CONCLUDING STATEMENT & FINAL THOUGHT

By proactively identifying and addressing process leaks using SOPs and SIPOC analysis, businesses can significantly enhance profitability and build a more resilient and sustainable operation. Remember, process excellence is about protecting existing revenue and preventing future losses, not just about generating more revenue.

Quote: *"Profits don't disappear overnight—they leak silently through unseen cracks in your process."*

Puzzle:

● **Profit Leak Detective:** A company has unexplained financial losses. What steps would you take to identify the source of the leaks?

Quiz:

- What are "silent profit killers"?

- Name three common operational process leaks.

- Name three common financial process leaks.

CHAPTER 8

Scaling for Success: Building Scalable Processes

INTRODUCTION

Many start-ups prioritize agility and rapid growth in their early stages, often neglecting the importance of establishing robust and scalable processes. This often leads to challenges as the company grows, with 23% of start-ups failing due to scaling issues (according to CB Insights). This chapter explores the critical link between process development and sustainable growth, outlining the key stages of business evolution and providing a roadmap for building scalable processes that support long-term success.

SECTION 1: THE GROWTH TRAP: WHY START-UPS FAIL TO SCALE

1.1. The Allure of Agility: A Double-Edged Sword

Start-ups often favour agility and adaptability, which are crucial in the early stages. However, a lack of structured processes can become a major obstacle as the company scales.

1.2. The High Cost of Poor Process Development

Poorly designed processes lead to inefficiencies, bottlenecks, and ultimately, failure.

→ **Increased Complexity:** As businesses grow, complexity increases exponentially, making it more challenging to manage processes effectively.

→ **Communication Breakdown:** Lack of clear processes leads to miscommunication, errors, and delays.

→ **Inconsistent Service Quality:** Inconsistencies in processes lead to inconsistent service quality, negatively impacting customer satisfaction.

1.3. Case Study: WeWork's Collapse – A Cautionary Tale

WeWork's rapid expansion without a solid financial and operational structure serves as a cautionary tale. Their failure to build robust processes resulted in a near-collapse.

SECTION 2: THE FOUR STAGES OF BUSINESS GROWTH AND PROCESS EVOLUTION

A Phased Approach to Scaling:

Sustainable growth requires a phased approach to process development, aligning processes with the company's evolving needs at each stage of growth.

2.1. Stage 1: Ideation and Launch

This stage focuses on adaptability, customer validation, and lean operations. Processes are flexible and iterative.

2.2. Stage 2: Early Growth

This stage prioritizes standardization of customer on boarding, hiring, and financial tracking. Processes become more defined and documented.

2.3. Stage 3: Expansion and Scaling

This stage emphasizes implementing Tech enablement, quality control, and scalable workflows. Processes are optimized for efficiency and growth.

2.4. Stage 4: Maturity and Optimization

This stage focuses on refinement, innovation, and long-term sustainability. Processes are continuously improved and adapted to changing market dynamics.

Case Study: Zappos's Successful Scaling

Zappos's remarkable growth illustrates how evolving processes and prioritizing customer service SOPs can drive sustainable scaling. They invested significantly in company culture and employee empowerment.

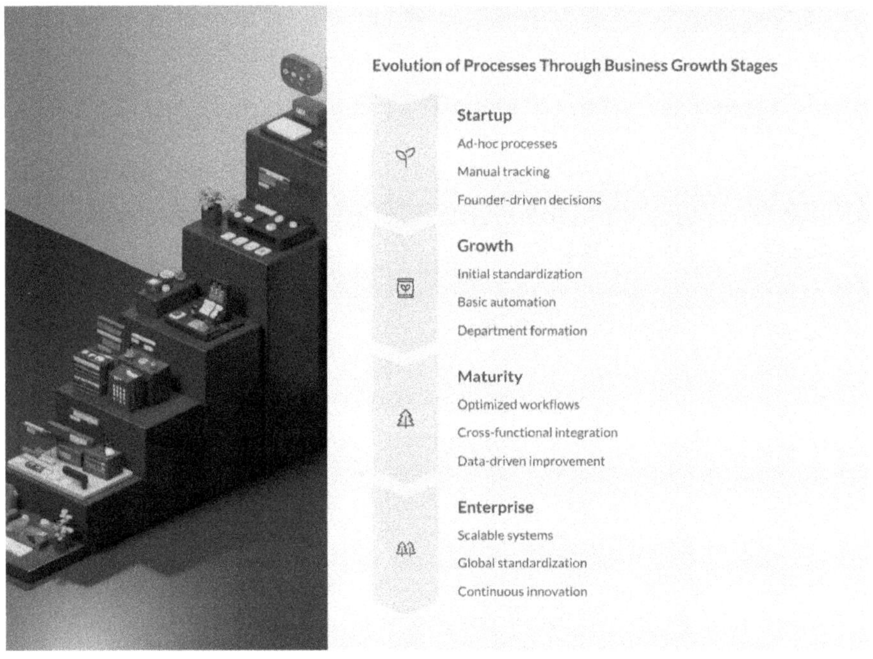

SECTION 3: PROCESS FRAMEWORKS THAT SUPPORT SCALING

This section discusses frameworks for supporting scalable processes.

→ **Lean and Agile:** Combines flexibility and structure.

→ **Process Automation:** Implementing efficiency-focused frameworks.

→ **SOPs and Protocols:** Documenting repeatable processes, ensuring consistency and quality.

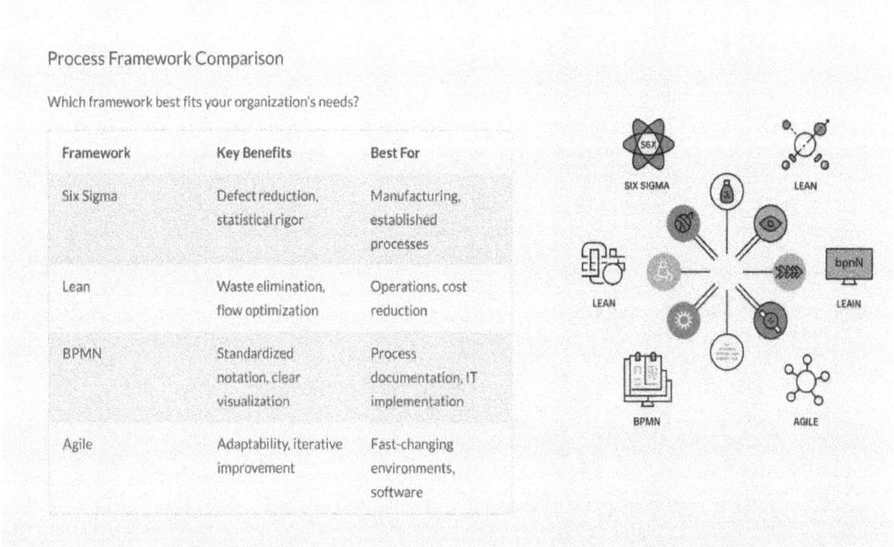

Framework	Key Benefits	Best For
Six Sigma	Defect reduction, statistical rigor	Manufacturing, established processes
Lean	Waste elimination, flow optimization	Operations, cost reduction
BPMN	Standardized notation, clear visualization	Process documentation, IT implementation
Agile	Adaptability, iterative improvement	Fast-changing environments, software

SECTION 5: PRACTICAL TOOLKIT: BUILDING SCALABLE PROCESSES

This section outlines important steps for building scalable processes:

→ **Start Early:** Design processes before chaos forces you to.

→ **Automate Wisely:** Leverage tools like HubSpot and Slack for efficiency.

→ **Review & Improve:** Adopt a mindset for continuous improvement.

→ **Train & Empower:** Scaling is about people, not just systems.

Concluding Statement & Final Thought

Building scalable processes is not merely about efficiency; it's about creating a foundation for sustainable growth and long-term success. By proactively designing and implementing robust processes, companies can navigate the challenges of scaling, avoiding common pitfalls and achieving sustained success.

Success Story: Reliance Jio's 4G Network Launch. This story effectively demonstrates how meticulously planned processes and technological investments allowed for rapid growth and market disruption. It showcases the importance of having robust, scalable processes in place for managing growth in a highly competitive industry. Their success was driven by highly planned processes, demonstrating the importance of forward-thinking and thorough process design before scaling.

Quote: *"What got you here won't take you there—unless your process evolves with your ambition."*

Quiz:

- What are some of the challenges of scaling?

- List the four stages of business growth and process evolution.

- Name three process frameworks that support scaling.

CHAPTER 9

The Power of Key Performance Indicators (KPIs): Measuring What Matters Most

INTRODUCTION

In today's data-driven world, many businesses fall into the trap of tracking countless Key Performance Indicators (KPIs), often focusing on vanity metrics that look good but don't drive results. This chapter cuts through the noise, identifying the essential KPIs that truly matter—the high-impact metrics that provide actionable insights and drive meaningful improvements in your processes and overall business performance.

SECTION 1: THE KPI OVERLOAD PROBLEM: WHY LESS IS MORE

1.1. The Pitfalls of KPI Overload

Tracking too many KPIs leads to decision fatigue, hindering effective decision-making. A Harvard Business Review study found that 70% of executives struggle with KPI overload.

Info source: HBR - Why KPIs Fail (https://hbr.org/2020/11/why-kpis-fail)

1.2. The Importance of Focus: Prioritizing High-Impact KPIs

Instead of tracking numerous metrics, focus on the vital few—the high-impact KPIs that directly drive business outcomes. This allows for more effective monitoring, analysis, and decision-making.

1.3. The Startup with 50+ Metrics

A Startup initially tracked 50+ metrics, yet struggled to identify critical issues and make data-driven decisions. In contrast to big established companies which focus on a small number of high-impact KPIs, providing a clear path for driving growth.

SECTION 2: THE 5 ESSENTIAL PROCESS KPIS

This section defines five essential process KPIs, explaining their importance and how they can be used for process optimization.

2.1. Efficiency Ratio (Output/Input)

This KPI measures the efficiency of resource utilization—how effectively time, money, and labour are converted into results.

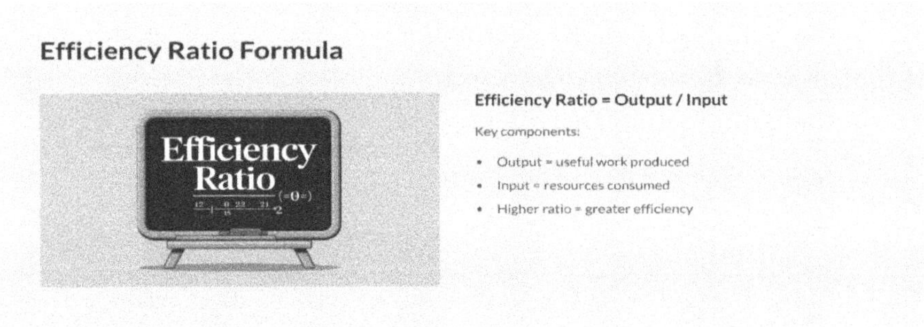

2.2. Cycle Time (Speed of Completion)

This KPI tracks the time taken from the start to the completion of a process. Optimizing cycle time is crucial for improving efficiency and customer satisfaction.

→ **Example:** Domino's 30-minute pizza delivery promise is built on cycle time optimization.

→ **Tip:** Use Lean / Six Sigma methods to identify bottlenecks and improve cycle time.

→ **Info source: Domino's Delivery Promise**

(https://www.dominos.com/en/about-dominos/our-story)

2.3. First-Time Right (Quality Without Rework)

This KPI measures the percentage of processes completed correctly the first time, minimizing errors and rework.

→ **Example:** Moglix enabled 100% "first-time-right" fabrication for a leading Indian natural resources conglomerate, eliminating rework and ensuring smooth capex project execution.

→ **Tip:** Integrated planning and quality checks at source significantly improve output accuracy and reduce costs.

→ **Source:** Moglix Case Study(https://business.moglix.com/case-studies)

2.4. Customer Impact Score

This KPI measures how a process affects the customer experience. It's crucial for optimizing processes to meet customer needs and expectations.

→ **Example:** Netflix measures browsing time before content selection, using this data to improve their recommendation algorithm.

→ **Pro Insight:** The most impactful process improvements often come from tracking customer friction points.

Info source: (https://research.netflix.com/research-area/machine-learning)

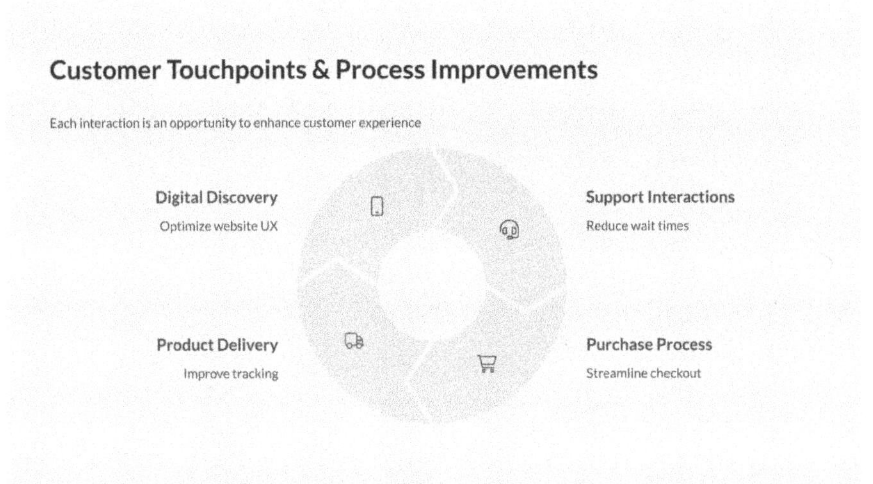

2.5. Cost-to-Value Ratio

This KPI compares process costs to the actual value generated. It's crucial for identifying cost-effective processes and maximizing profitability.

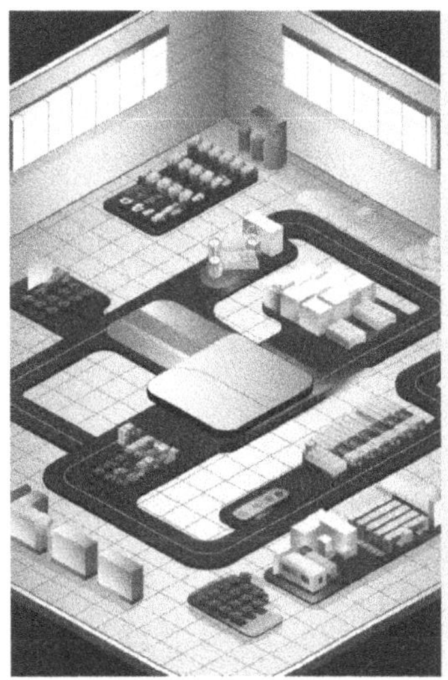

Apple's strategy balances high quality components with tightly controlled manufacturing.

Process	Cost Factor	Value Ratio
Just-in-time inventory	Low storage costs	5:1 return
Vertical integration	High initial investment	7:1 return

SECTION 3: COMMON KPI MISTAKES AND HOW TO AVOID THEM

This section identifies common mistakes in KPI tracking and provides practical advice on avoiding them.

→ **KPI Overload:** Tracking too many KPIs leads to decision fatigue. Use the "So What?" test – if a KPI doesn't lead to action, discard it.

→ **Activity vs. Results:** Focus on leading indicators that predict success rather than simply measuring activity.

SECTION 4: KPI DASHBOARDS: TRACKING AND ACTING ON DATA

This section explains how to use KPI dashboards to visualize and analyse data.

→ **Visualization Tools:** Use tools like Power BI, Tableau, or Google Data Studio.

→ **Example:** Airbnb tracks cancellation rates to improve host reliability and customer experience.

→ **Action Plan:** Set KPI review cycles (daily, weekly, monthly) to ensure adaptability.

Info source: (https://www.rentalscaleup.com/airbnb-professional-tools-discover-the-new-airbnb-performance-report-tab-and-its-quality-metrics)

SECTION 5: IMPORTANT KPI'S FOR DIFFERENT BUSINESS ROLES

This section provides tailored KPI recommendations for different roles.

→ **Entrepreneurs:** Revenue per employee, customer churn, cost of acquisition.

→ **Corporates:** Operational efficiency, compliance adherence, employee productivity.

→ **Sales & Marketing Teams:** Conversion rates, lead quality scores, customer lifetime value.

Concluding Statement & Final Thought

KPIs are your business pulse. By focusing on the essential few and using data-driven decision-making, businesses can achieve significant improvements in efficiency, profitability, and customer satisfaction.

Airbnb's Success Story. Airbnb's focus on improving host verification and customer service KPIs contributed to their remarkable growth and success. This illustrates the importance of tracking customer-centric metrics and making data-driven decisions. The story showcases how prioritizing a few key performance indicators, and the strategic use of data to make improvements, directly contributed to their business success.

Quote: *"Not everything that counts can be measured—but what you measure must count."*

Puzzle:

- **KPI Prioritization:** You can only track three KPIs for your customer service team. Which three would you choose and why?

Quiz:

- What is "KPI overload," and why is it a problem?

- Name five essential process KPIs.

- What are some common mistakes in KPI tracking?

CHAPTER 10

The 1% Rule: Unlocking Exponential Growth Through Small, Consistent Improvements

INTRODUCTION

Dramatic breakthroughs are often celebrated, but sustained success is rarely built on singular, monumental achievements. Instead, it's the accumulation of small, consistent improvements that fuels exponential growth. This chapter explores the philosophy of continuous improvement, demonstrating how small, incremental changes, implemented consistently, can lead to remarkable results over time.

SECTION 1: RULE POWER

1.1. Continuous Improvement in Action

This emphasizes the power of making tiny, consistent improvements daily. The cumulative effect of these seemingly small gains is exponential growth over time.

1.2. The Mathematics of Marginal Gains: Compounding Growth

A 1% daily improvement compounds over time, leading to a 37x improvement over a year. This illustrates the significant impact of consistently making small improvements.

SECTION 2: CASE STUDIES

2.1. International: Toyota – The Kaizen Culture

- **Toyota:** Its culture focuses on continuous small tweaks in its assembly-line processes. The cumulative impact of these small improvements has been remarkable, resulting in reduced defects, improved fuel efficiency, and increased output over decades.

2.2. India: Zerodha – Digital Transformation Through Incremental Improvements

- This Indian stockbroker achieved exponential growth through small, consistent improvements to its UI/UX, on boarding process, and customer support.

SECTION 3: THE SCIENCE BEHIND THE RULE: THE POWER OF COMPOUNDING

The Aggregation of Marginal Gains

The 1% rule highlights the power of compounding: Small, consistent improvements accumulate over time, leading to significant results. This concept is sometimes referred to as the "aggregation of marginal gains."

SECTION 4: FINAL ACTION

4.1. For Start-ups and Entrepreneurs

- **Optimize On boarding Flows:** Reduce friction to improve user experience.

- **Improve Customer Retention:** Target a 1% monthly improvement in retention.

- **Example:** Swiggy streamlined delivery time tracking, leading to faster service and lower costs.

4.2. For Corporates and Process Managers

- **Eliminate Bottlenecks:** Reduce manual interventions step by step.

4.3. For Individuals and Professionals

- **Improve Email Efficiency:** Increase response times by 1%.

- **Reduce Decision Fatigue:** Eliminate one minor decision per day.

SECTION 5: THE 1% GROWTH FRAMEWORK

- **Step 1:** Identify a process to improve.

- **Step 2:** Identify a small, incremental improvement (1% tweak).

- **Step 3:** Track and measure the impact (using KPIs).

- **Step 4:** Scale and repeat the improvement.

CONCLUDING STATEMENT & FINAL THOUGHT

The 1% rule is not about radical change; it's about consistent, incremental improvement. By embracing the Kaizen philosophy and focusing on small, consistent tweaks, businesses and individuals can unlock remarkable growth and achieve sustained success.

Let us summarize and understand the chapter through a beautiful story

Driving Excellence: Mahindra & Mahindra's Journey of Incremental Improvements

In the bustling corridors of Mahindra & Mahindra's manufacturing units, a quiet transformation was taking place. Faced with the challenges of increasing productivity, reducing costs, and enhancing quality, the company embarked on a journey of continuous, incremental improvements.

The Challenge: Enhancing Productivity and Efficiency

Mahindra & Mahindra identified several areas within their machine shop operations that required optimization. Manual cleaning operations, inefficient layouts, and underutilized machinery were contributing to bottlenecks, increased operational costs, and safety concerns.

The Strategy: Implementing Frugal and Lean Approaches

Embracing a frugal approach, the company undertook a comprehensive analysis of their operations. Key strategies included:

→ **Layout Optimization**: Reconfiguring the machine shop layout to streamline workflows and reduce unnecessary movement.

→ **Elimination of Manual Processes**: Replacing manual cleaning operations with automated solutions to enhance efficiency and safety.

→ **Equipment Utilization**: Maximizing the use of existing machinery by increasing the capacity of Vertical Turning Centres (VTCs) and eliminating underperforming machines.

→ **Lean Tools Application**: Implementing tools such as 5S, Poka-Yoke, and Value Stream Mapping to identify and eliminate waste.

The Impact: Tangible Improvements Across Key Metrics

The cumulative effect of these micro-optimizations led to significant improvements:

→ **Productivity**: Machine shop productivity improved drastically, effectively increasing the output without additional capital investment.

→ **Quality**: Enhanced processes led to better product quality, reducing defects and rework.

→ **Cost Reduction**: Operational costs decreased significantly, contributing to improved profitability.

→ **Delivery Time**: Streamlined operations resulted in significant reduction in delivery times.

→ **Safety and Morale**: Improved ergonomics and safer work environments boosted employee morale and reduced workplace incidents.

CONCLUSION: THE POWER OF INCREMENTAL GAINS

Mahindra & Mahindra's experience underscores the transformative power of focusing on small, continuous improvements. By meticulously analysing and refining each aspect of their operations, the company achieved substantial gains in productivity, quality, and efficiency. This case serves as a testament to how the philosophy of marginal gains can be effectively applied beyond sports, driving excellence in the manufacturing sector.

Info source: (https://www.slideshare.net/slideshow/application-of-frugal-approach-for-productivity-improvement-a-case-study-of-mahindra-and-mahindra-ltd/252259723)

Quote: "Small daily improvements are the compound interest of process excellence."

Quiz:

- What is the Kaizen philosophy?
- What is the mathematics of marginal gains?
- List the four steps of the 1% growth framework.

CHAPTER 11

Cultivating a Process Mastery Culture: The Key to Sustainable Success

INTRODUCTION

While exceptional individuals can make a significant difference, sustained business success hinges on more than individual talent. It depends on creating a culture that prioritizes and fosters process excellence. This chapter explores the core elements of a process-driven culture, demonstrating how organizations can shift from a people-dependent to a process-driven model, unlocking improved efficiency, scalability, and long-term success. Research shows that 85% of business failures stem from poor processes, not poor people.

SECTION 1: WHY PROCESS-DRIVEN CULTURES OUTPERFORM PEOPLE-DEPENDENT ONES

1.1. The Limitations of a People-Dependent Culture

Dependence on individual brilliance is inherently unsustainable. The departure of key employees often results in a significant loss of institutional knowledge and expertise. Without standardized processes, performance remains inconsistent and difficult to scale.

1.2. The Power of Process-Driven Cultures

A process-driven culture prioritizes process excellence, building repeatable, scalable, and robust systems. It ensures consistent performance, regardless of individual employee changes.

1.3. Case Study: Nokia vs. Apple

Nokia's dependence on a people-driven culture, in contrast to Apple's process-driven approach, highlights a crucial strategic difference. Apple's commitment to building repeatable processes in design and innovation has been a key driver of its sustained success.

Info source: BBC News - How Nokia lost its handset crown

Harvard Business Review - How Apple is Organized for Innovation

SECTION 2: THE FIVE PILLARS OF A PROCESS-DRIVEN CULTURE

This section outlines the key elements of a process-driven culture.

2.1. Standardization and Consistency

Standardized processes ensure predictable outcomes, reducing variability and errors.

2.2. Continuous Improvement

Foster a culture of continuous improvement, encouraging employees to suggest enhancements and make incremental improvements over time.

2.3. Empowered Teams

Empower employees to take ownership of processes, contributing ideas for improvement.

2.4. Data-Driven Decision-Making

Use process KPIs to monitor performance, identify bottlenecks, and make data-driven decisions.

2.5. Scalability and Resilience

Processes should be adaptable and scalable to support growth and handle unexpected challenges.

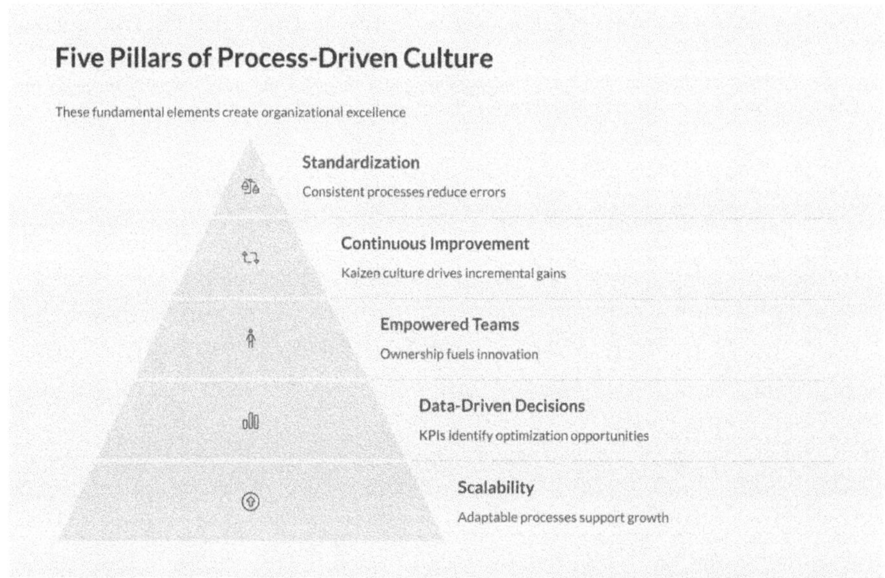

SECTION 3: GLOBAL PROCESS MASTERY: LESSONS FROM LEADING COMPANIES

This section showcases how leading companies have achieved process mastery.

3.1. The OKR System for Innovation

Google's Objectives and Key Results (OKRs) framework aligns all employees with company goals, driving efficiency without stifling innovation.

Info source: Chapter 2 of book " **Measure What Matters** written by John Doerr's

3.2. Customer Obsession Through Lean Processes

Amazon's customer-centric approach, combined with lean principles, optimizes processes for speed and efficiency. The 1-click checkout process is a prime example.

Info source: Amazon's 1-Click Patent (started in 1999 expired in 2017)

Amazon's Leadership Principles

SECTION 4: HOW TO EMBED A PROCESS MASTERY CULTURE IN YOUR ORGANIZATION

This section provides a practical, five-step framework for creating a process-driven culture.

- → **Step 1:** Clearly define core processes (document SOPs, automate where possible).

- → **Step 2:** Create a mindset (encourage daily improvements).

- → **Step 3:** Align teams with business goals (use OKRs, Six Sigma).

- → **Step 4:** Leverage technology and digitization.

- → **Step 5:** Reward process excellence.

Concluding Statement & Final Thought

A strong process culture is not merely a set of best practices; it is the foundation for sustainable success. By embracing the principles of process mastery, businesses can unlock greater efficiency, resilience, and scalability, outperforming their competitors in the long run.

Quote: "Culture eats strategy for breakfast—but only if your processes make room at the table."

Quiz:

- What are the limitations of a people-dependent culture?

- What are the five pillars of a process-driven culture?

- Name three companies that have achieved process mastery.

CHAPTER 12

The Future of Process Excellence – Embracing AI and Automation

A GLIMPSE INTO TOMORROW

The future of process excellence is no longer a question of "if," but "how fast." Organizations that delay the adoption of AI and automation may soon find themselves outpaced, outperformed, and ultimately out of the race. As digital transformation accelerates, intelligent technologies are not just support tools—they are becoming the new engine rooms of operational excellence. This chapter explores how process excellence is evolving through the power of AI and automation and what it means for tomorrow's organizations.

SECTION 1: THE INEVITABLE SHIFT TO DIGITAL PROCESS EXCELLENCE

1.1. The Competitive Edge

Artificial Intelligence (AI) and automation are ushering in a new era of intelligent decision-making and seamless execution. From analysing complex datasets in real-time to executing tasks with unmatched precision, these tools have reshaped how organizations define "efficiency."

Where traditional process improvement took weeks of brainstorming and audits, AI-driven systems now deliver insights instantly—pinpointing friction points, forecasting failures, and suggesting the optimal next move.

1.2. The Urgency to Adapt

The window to adapt is shrinking. As customer expectations evolve and competition intensifies, organizations are under pressure to deliver faster, smarter, and more personalized experiences. Automation isn't a luxury—it's the foundation for staying relevant in a rapidly digitizing world. Companies must shift from a reactive to a proactive mindset, embedding adaptability and intelligence into their DNA.

SECTION 2: NEXT-GENERATION TOOLS DRIVING TRANSFORMATION

The backbone of digital process excellence lies in emerging technologies that simplify complexity, enhance precision, and scale performance without proportionally increasing costs.

2.1. AI-Powered Process Mining & Optimization

Process mining tools powered by AI scan operational data trails across departments. They uncover hidden inefficiencies, deviations, and bottlenecks—offering visual maps of what is really happening in processes versus what was designed. These tools not only diagnose problems but also recommend and implement optimizations dynamically.

2.2. Robotic Process Automation (RPA) & Hyper automation

RPA automates rule-based, repetitive tasks, freeing human resources for higher-value work. When combined with AI and analytics in a hyper automation ecosystem, organizations can automate even decision-based processes, orchestrating seamless end-to-end workflows.

2.3. Intelligent Chabot's & Virtual Assistants

Conversational AI has moved beyond simple Q&A bots. Today's virtual assistants support internal approvals, financial reconciliations, appointment scheduling, and even on boarding—providing real-time support to both customers and employees while continuously learning and evolving.

2.4. Smart Workflow Optimization & Real-Time Monitoring

The integration of connected devices and sensors with automation platforms has transformed how operations are monitored. Data collected in real-time is now fed into predictive analytics engines, allowing for preventive actions, optimized maintenance schedules, and agile process adjustments—all driven by AI.

SECTION 3: USE CASES AND APPLICATION AREAS (GENERIC VIEW)

AI and automation are no longer confined to tech labs—they're actively shaping outcomes across business functions:

→ **In Operations**: Workflow orchestration and real-time decision support systems reduce delays, waste, and human errors.

→ **In Human Resources**: AI matches talent to roles based on skill compatibility and predictive attrition modelling, creating smarter hiring pipelines.

→ **In Customer Experience**: Predictive models help pre-empt customer concerns, tailoring responses and offers for improved satisfaction and loyalty.

→ **In Finance & Compliance**: Intelligent systems flag anomalies, ensure real-time regulatory compliance, and automate risk-based scoring models.

→ **In Logistics & Supply Chain**: AI-driven demand forecasting aligns procurement and inventory levels with real-time needs, improving delivery and reducing excess.

SECTION 4: CHALLENGES IN ADOPTING AI AND AUTOMATION

Despite its transformative potential, the journey toward intelligent process excellence is not without roadblocks:

→ **Initial Investment Costs**: While long-term savings are significant, upfront investment in technology and training can be a deterrent.

→ **Workforce Resistance**: Change is uncomfortable. Teams may fear displacement or struggle to adapt to digital workflows.

→ **Security and Data Privacy Risks**: As more systems become interconnected, protecting sensitive information and maintaining regulatory compliance becomes critical.

→ **Skill Gaps**: Successful adoption requires cross-functional teams trained in both domain knowledge and data literacy.

→ **Ethical Considerations**: Ensuring fairness, transparency, and accountability in AI-driven decision-making is vital to building trust.

Section 5: The Future Ahead – Trends Reshaping Excellence

Looking ahead, organizations will need to evolve into **intelligent ecosystems** where automation doesn't just support operations—it **steers them.**

→ **AI-First Autonomous Enterprises**: Businesses will rely on AI to make autonomous operational and strategic decisions.

→ **Hyper-Personalized Experiences**: Using behavioural data and context, AI will predict and deliver hyper-customized services and offerings.

→ **Quantum-Assisted Optimization**: The use of quantum computing for solving complex, multi-variable problems will revolutionize supply chain management, resource allocation, and even fraud detection.

→ **Ethical AI Governance**: There will be a growing emphasis on responsible AI frameworks to ensure fairness, transparency, and inclusivity in automated decisions.

→ **Digital Twins & Simulation-Driven Planning**: Businesses will create real-time digital replicas of entire processes or systems, using them to simulate future outcomes and optimize before real-world execution.

CONCLUDING THOUGHT – ADAPT TO EVOLVE

The journey of process excellence is entering a new chapter—one driven by intelligence, agility, and automation. While the tools have changed, the goal remains timeless: to deliver better, faster, and smarter outcomes. The organizations that embrace this shift—not just in tools but in mindset—will not only survive the next wave of disruption but lead it.

The future isn't waiting. The question is—are you ready to transform before you're forced to?

Quote: "Tomorrow's leaders won't just adapt to automation—they'll architect it."

Quiz:

- What is the competitive advantage of AI-driven automation?

- Name four next-generation process tools.

- What are some of the challenges in AI and automation adoption?

Closing Note – The Final Page is Just the Beginning

As you close this book, I want you to pause and reflect—not just on what you've read, but on what's possible from here.

Just like the human body doesn't stop functioning after one task is done—your heart continues to beat, your lungs continue to breathe, your mind continues to think—**process mastery is not a one-time achievement; it's a lifelong rhythm.**

You now hold in your hands more than a playbook. You hold a mindset, a philosophy, a lens through which to see order where others see confusion. Where others see chaos, you now have the clarity to design.

You've learned to structure workflows like arteries channelling life, to detox inefficiencies like kidneys filtering waste, and to keep the pulse of progress alive just as the heart never takes a break.

You've become more than a professional.

You've become a **Process Master.**

But mastery isn't a destination—it's a choice you make every day.

In how you lead.

In how you execute.

In how you think.

And in how you inspire others to rise.

So whether you're redesigning a system, mentoring a team, or building something from the ground up—know this:

You were never meant to manage chaos. You were meant to master it.

Thank you for allowing me to be a part of your journey. I hope this book empowers you not just to build better businesses, but to live with more intention, discipline, and flow—in every process, and in every part of life.

"We are what we repeatedly do. Excellence, then, is not an act, but a habit." — Aristotle

और अंत में दिल से निकली कुछ पंक्तियाँ:

«मंज़िलें मिलती हैं उन्हीं को जो राहों का हुनर रखते हैं,

वो कई बार गिरते हैं, पर फिर भी सफ़र रखते हैं।

प्रोसेस बनाकर जो काम करें, वो बेहतर नतीजा लाते हैं,

क्योंकि जो चलते हैं सिलसिले से — वही नए रास्ते पाते हैं।"

"Destinations are reached by those who know how to walk the path,

They may fall often, yet they continue their journey.

Those who follow a process achieve better outcomes,

For those who walk with rhythm—find new roads ahead."